THE PSYCHOLOGY OF HANDWRITING
Secrets of Handwriting Analysis

By NADYA OLYANOVA

Published by
Melvin Powers
WILSHIRE BOOK COMPANY
12015 Sherman Road
No. Hollywood, California 91605
Telephone: (213) 875-1711 / (818) 983-1105

Printed by

HAL LEIGHTON PRINTING COMPANY
P.O. Box 3952
North Hollywood, California 91605
Telephone: (213) 983-1105

To Vitorio Korjhan

Have we not all, amid life's petty strife,
Some pure ideal of a noble life
That once seemed possible? Did we not hear
The flutter of its wings, and feel it near
And just within our reach? It was. And yet
We lost it in this daily jar and fret.
But still our place is kept, and it will wait,
Ready for us to fill it, soon or late.
No star was ever lost we once have seen;
We always may be what we might have been.
—ADELAIDE PROCTOR

Manufactured in the United States of America
Library of Congress Catalog Card No.: 59-13005

ISBN 0-87980-128-X

Grateful Acknowledgment

To George E. Edington and Bradford J. Wilson, my former pupils, who seem to have outrun their teacher in many respects and for whose devoted assistance I cannot express my gratitude.

To Eleanor Reese and Mary Hambidge whose encouragement during a critical period bolstered my spirit.

To Dr. Harmon S. Ephron whose patience, understanding and sense of humor oiled the wheels which had become rusty and who wrote the introduction to this book.

To my many friends, too numerous to mention, for their acts of kindness and friendship before and during the writing of this book, who will know I mean them when they read this.

And last but not least, to my late husband, William N. Caruthers, who—wherever he is—knows that I have accomplished at last what, for years, he encouraged me to do.

To My Readers

Your destiny is in your handwriting because it expresses the *real* you: your ambitions, fantasies, goals, talents. It reveals your frustrations; what you *are* and what you *might have been*. Best of all, it gives you clues to what you *still* can be!

Who of us has not felt at one time or another that, had the fates been kinder, we could have been *more* than what we are? What happened to your childhood dreams which seemed to vanish with the years, you know not why or where?

You can recapture those early dreams, recognize *why* they drifted into nothingness, and *do* something toward realizing them.

Dr. Alfred Adler, the Viennese psychologist, once said: "Handwriting is frozen motion." Transform it, then, into a productive thaw and let your talents, as they are revealed in your handwriting, lead you into fields of creative self-expression.

Nadya Olyanova

Contents

Introduction

It is part of the human condition that we are all born with a deep need to communicate—to share our thoughts, feelings and experiences with other human beings. For this reason, the way we speak, the way we dress and even our most subtle changes of posture or facial expression are all part of the hidden language we use to tell the world who we are and what we are.

Careful observers like Freud have helped us to understand just how far-reaching and basic are the dynamics which underlie some minor point of self-expression. Events which on the surface may seem trivial or inconsequential can often convey a whole world of meaning to the careful observer. It is not surprising then that our *handwriting*, which characterizes each of us as an individual, should reveal so much about our life activities and our behavioral patterns.

The trained psychiatrist learns to sense the undercurrents in personality. Over the years he will usually become adept at catching small clues which lead him to evaluate the patient on a level not revealed on the surface. He can always, however, use supplementary evaluative techniques, and often calls for them.

In my clinical practice I have learned that no one is infallible. A second professional opinion is frequently useful. The bright, cheerful patient, for example, who comes into my office radiating charm and good humor may sometimes be hiding morbid, bizarre or destructive thoughts. The sooner I know about these problems, the sooner I can help start the troubled person on the road to a healthy, balanced, mature life.

A deceptive situation may likewise occur when an obviously disturbed person conceals unsuspected drives and resources for health. In such a case the initial interview could leave me in some doubt as to the patient's available reserves of strength. At such times a psychologist's report, based on thorough and expert testing, is usually helpful. It can throw considerable light on hitherto unrevealed capacities (or weaknesses, as the case may be). In addition to the variety of tests given by psychologists, I like to include a handwriting evaluation by a competent graphologist.

It often happens that in critical situations I do not have time for thorough psychological testing. When this is the case, a few lines of handwriting and a signature will enable me to obtain a brief but useful psychological report in as little as two hours. Lest anyone doubt the validity of such psychological findings, it may be added that subsequent testing, by top-ranking psychologists, has yielded reports which have invariably tallied with those of the expert graphologist.

Graphology has an added, unique advantage. It yields a vivid picture of patients or their relatives, who, for one reason or another, cannot be given the usual tests. This is of special help when the parents of a patient live too far away to cooperate in the treatment.

In the clinical reports that Nadya Olyanova has prepared for me and for other psychiatrists, she explores the full range of personality, and impressively demonstrates the extent of her insights, experience, learning and good common sense. While she insists that anyone can learn the techniques of graphology, it is quite evident that her own considerable skill is the result of persistent study, great gifts of understanding, unusual talent, and tireless devotion to her profession.

She has studied with pioneers in the field of graphology, and thanks to her remarkable sensitivity to the ways of the human psyche, she is today among the top-ranking graphologists in the country. She commands respect particularly for her profound sense of devotion to graphology as a clinical tool, rather than a "game" for parlor amusement. She has always been an enthusiastic teacher, and has ably instructed classes of physician-students of psychotherapy and psychoanalysis. She has stimulated psychiatrists and psychologists to study and use graphology as an important clinical indicator of trends in their patients' progress.

Like all approaches to human understanding, graphology, among the other projective studies of psychodynamics, has had to battle for recognition. The fact that today it has become an increasingly acceptable part of the psychologist's armamentarium is due to the diligence, integrity and enthusiasm of such workers as the writer of this volume.

Harmon S. Ephron, M.D.

1. By Their Handwritings You Shall Know Them

One trait many of us have in common is that of labelling people. We pigeonhole our friends and so-called enemies—the latter in none too flattering terms. John is a bore, Mildred a snob, Helen a pseudo intellectual. That loud-mouthed fellow who insists on monopolizing the conversation and hogs the spotlight you call an egomaniac. And Grace, you say, is antisocial because she wears a smirk on her face and never seems to have a kind word for anyone.

Then there's Paul, whom you've always considered peculiar. Most of the time he has a chip on his shoulder, arguing at the drop of a hat and antagonizing everyone he meets. A few drinks and he becomes violent, insulting the friends who are kindest to him. If you're familiar with the language of psychology you may label him a "psychopath," "schizophrenic" or "manic-depressive."

It might surprise you to discover that your pat estimates of these people are not basically sound because you are judging them super-ficially.

"Could be," you admit reluctantly, "but what *is* a sure-fire way of getting the real low-down?"

The answer is comparatively simple because all these people *write*. It's their *handwritings* which will give you true pictures of what they really are. And you can take a closer look at yourself, through your own handwriting, too.

Of course, you will have to learn to estimate carefully; to balance negative features against positive ones, strength against weakness. You may discover traits, attributes and talents you never suspected existed in these people you thought you knew so well. With your own writing as a guide, too, you may discover potentials within yourself that you weren't aware of, characteristics to be strengthened or perhaps eliminated.

If you have letters written by some of your friends, dig them out. Spread them in front of you as you might their photographs. The first thing you will see is how different one is from the other. There may be resemblances but there are no two exactly alike. You already know that these people differ in temperament, intellect, abilities. Now you can learn the cause of the differences and what they really mean. After some practice you'll begin to recognize the clues to their unique personalities, and knowing the reasons for them may make you drop your old labels and re-evaluate your friends. As your knowledge of graphology grows, you will gain more and more insights into what makes people tick.

Through the handwritings of your men and women friends, you can choose a harmonious group with common interests to invite to your home for a stimulating evening. You can learn how best to get along with your husband, wife, relatives, or the person you are considering for marriage. Anyone who arouses in you more than just a passing interest can be better understood through an analysis of his or her handwriting. And you can be more constructive in helping your friends through your understanding, instead of giving the kind of criticism that might prove destructive and drive many of them away.

You'll find answers to many questions in the handwritings of people who cross your path daily—your employer, the girl in your office with whom you can't seem to get along, your neighbors, your lawyer, even your psychiatrist, if you have one. At the same time you will attain a better understanding of yourself. You'll be confronted with a glaring, unvarnished picture of the real you, and if you can take what you see, you can consider yourself mature!

The handwritings used in this book are analyzed briefly. To give you a complete verbal picture of even one of them might take an entire chapter. You will find among them examples of the various types of people in many walks of life. None of us is a *pure* type. For instance, the "career woman" might be a strong mixture of the homemaker and capable business executive, managing her personal life so efficiently that she can hold a responsible job even while she is raising a family with its attendant domestic duties. The businessman may have the qualities of the artist in him, and paint pictures or write stories in his spare time.

The introvert may possess a number of extroverted qualities, appearing positive and forceful to the outside world, when he is really a mouse at heart and under the control of a devouring, possessive woman!

Perhaps you have known someone who was always ready with a humorous joke or quip, until his attempt at suicide made you wonder what unhappiness drove him to such despair. Could you have known that his cheerful exterior was just a façade to cover up his inner feelings of hopelessness? His handwriting would reveal the warning signals of attempted suicide, though it might also indicate his sense of humor. (Yes, morbid people often have a good sense of humor. What saves them is that they *can* laugh at themselves.)

With practice, your eye will learn to recognize the signs in handwriting, explained in detail in this book, and you will remember their meanings. This will give you new and interesting insights into the characters of those who write to you, whether in a love letter, an application for a job or a note left in haste by a neighbor.

You will get to the point where you will know whether someone is telling you the truth or a white lie to prevent your feelings from being hurt. You will quickly recognize the writer of a letter from the handwritten address on the envelope. (You probably already can tell without knowing anything about graphology. This is because you are a visual type. If you weren't, you wouldn't be interested, in the first place, in looking at handwriting.)

You may discover that you have been misjudging some of your friends and associates and have been correct about others. Perhaps *your* handwriting will reveal the signs of the natural psychologist. How can you tell? Look for indications of intuition, good judgment, imagination coupled with a real interest in people. If the sign of altruism shows, too, then your graphological preoccupation will put you in a position to help others understand themselves better.

Remember to be charitable. Don't judge too hastily, if you must judge at all. Follow the rules carefully when analyzing a handwriting, and make one rule for yourself: *don't make a statement unless you are reasonably certain it is correct!*

2. What Is Graphology?

". . . the art or science of deducing character, disposition or aptitudes from handwriting." —WEBSTER

How It Began

Legend tells us that writing was first begun by the ancient Egyptian god Thoth, who is pictured with the face of the sacred bird, the ibis. In his hands he holds a "pen"—a flat reed crushed to the softness of a brush. Thoth, the story goes, scratched his bill in the muddy banks of the Nile—and writing was born.

Thoth

The word *graphology* was coined from the Greek *graph* which means *writing* and the suffix *ology* which is applied to names of scientific studies.

As early as the 11th century, a Chinese philosopher and painter named Jo-Hau declared that "Handwriting infallibly shows us whether it comes from a vulgar or noble-minded person."

In 1622 Camillo Baldi, doctor and professor at the University of Bologna, and a famous scholar of his day, asserted that it was obvious that all persons wrote in their own peculiar way and that in private letters everyone used characteristic forms which could not be truly imitated by anyone else.

The artist Gainsborough invariably kept before him, while he was working on a portrait, the handwriting of his subject.

A revealing reference is made about the importance of handwriting in Stevenson's *Dr. Jekyll and Mr. Hyde*. It was, in fact, the handwriting of Hyde which Mr. Utterson the lawyer spoke about to his clerk Mr. Guest, whom he described as "a great student and critic of handwriting." Comparing Hyde's handwriting with that of Dr. Jekyll's, the clerk said: "There is a singular resemblance; the two hands are in many points identical, only differently sloped."

Aesop, Aristotle, Julius Caesar and Cicero were among the outstanding personalities of ancient days who advocated the study of handwriting in order to know the character of a person. Later students of graphology were Sir Walter Scott, Disraeli and Robert Browning.

Thus, over a period of many hundreds of years, men and women of intellect and intuition used handwriting as a means of judging character. From their intuitive findings a set of rules developed and it is by these that the student of graphology is guided today.

The Influence of Training

Early in the 20th century, a form of writing called the Palmer Method came into prominence and was taught in the elementary schools. It followed the ornate Spencerian hand—was, in fact, a refinement of it, and was designed to make the penmanship of school children legible and beautiful. The child who rebelled against schoolroom routine—or for that matter against any set rules laid down by authority—broke away from the set forms taught him and developed a characteristically individual handwriting of his own. Many children retained the Palmer formations of letters and words even into adulthood and we still see signs of them today.

Both the Spencerian and Palmer Methods of writing reflected the spirit, the style (even of dress), of their times. Then came a period of progress and greater cultural development, and this was reflected in manuscript writing which was being taught in progressive and private schools. This method—a form of printing—is still in use today in such schools and reflects greater aesthetic development. (Printing usually points up the aesthetic and/or artistic elements in an individual's make-up.)

National Characteristics

Every nation has its characteristic hand. English writing is recognized readily by the vertical angle of reserve, by old-fashioned capital letters which reveal respect for old traditions, and by use of the underscored signature, which expresses the writer's façade of superiority as compensation for a basic inferiority complex.

The Spanish hand is distinguished by its expression of old-world pride in large, old-fashioned, dignified capital letters; by intense emotionality kept rigidly under control, which is revealed in heavy pen pressure coupled with closeness of letter forms, often quite angular.

The American hand, characteristically, is that of the salesman type, indicated by signs of aggressiveness in t bars which slant downward and by long lower loops expressing materialism. Essentially the writing flows to the right, a sign of the extroversion of the salesman.

Handwriting and Personality

Character traits change in individuals as changes take place in a culture. These changes reveal themselves in handwriting, even though it takes a long time for a new set of ideas or habits to wear a groove in one's inner consciousness. If an individual's handwriting shows a receptivity to new experiences and changes, an examination of specimens written over a period of years will clearly show the person's development (or regression). (See "The Evolution of a Personality," page 149.)

The way in which the individual writes, just as the manner in which he shakes hands, laughs, walks, and makes unconscious gestures, tells you much more than his words alone. Handwriting is a composite

14

picture of the way a person's mind works, how his thinking affects his emotions, what his attitude is toward life and other human beings. It is, as one psychology professor described it, *congealed integrated behavior.*

In Europe, and especially Germany, graphology has always been studied in connection with the subject of psychology. In the United States it has been taken less seriously until the recent arrival of many students of this science. Slowly but surely, it is moving into the realm where it belongs as a valuable psychometric tool in assisting psychiatrists and psychologists in their diagnoses. Along with other projective techniques, such as the Rorschach Ink Blot Test, an analysis of a subject's handwriting is being used to throw further light on his character structure and certain habit patterns which may not be readily discerned by other tests.

Graphology has also come to be used as an aid in vocational guidance for students entering upon careers; in personnel selection for business firms and banks; and in discerning whether men and women are suited for each other in marriage.

The evidence is clear that we are moving forward graphologically. It is welcome progress, for the study of handwriting is a step in helping to discover the truth about ourselves, and only in knowing the truth can we be truly free.

What Handwriting Does Not Reveal

The *sex*—whether male or female—is not revealed in handwriting. Neither is the *age* of the writer.

What a person does—the work he is engaged in—does not usually show, although potentialities for what he can do are revealed. On the other hand, some occupations do influence handwriting (just as they influence the writers' points of view) and the expert often recognizes the handwriting of the bookkeeper, the engineer and the artist.

Criminal tendencies will be revealed to the practiced eye of the graphologist, but the *criminal,* per se, cannot be detected. Who of us is not capable of an act of violence if sufficiently driven by intense emotional fervor? I have in mind the handwriting of a prisoner I once examined—a man who had killed his wife when he found her in the arms of her lover. His handwriting revealed him to be a mild little man, and this same mildness was the façade he showed to the world. Only signs of temper gave the clue to his violent act—a temper which was

15

slow to grow but reached the extreme of insanity at its peak. He probably would never commit another act of violence.

The Writer's Sex

Why can't we tell a person's sex from handwriting? In all of us there are both masculine and feminine components which have nothing to do with physiology.

We have all met a man we considered feminine or effeminate. We may have labelled him a "fussy old woman," or even branded him homosexual.

By the same token, there is the woman whose manner, dress, choice of work have caused us to regard her as masculine. Why? What are the traits that have come to be accepted as masculine, and what are thought of as feminine? It is a difficult question, because our culture, a succession of wars, the influence of the machine, all have had a share in bringing out either masculine or feminine traits in each of us. There are few of us who can be considered "typically male" or "typically female," unless we think of the stereotyped "homebody" as essentially feminine, and the manual laborer as the representative of masculinity.

Experiments with children have shown that little girls in their formative years have enjoyed being tied up by little boys, while little boys enjoyed tying them up. Does this mean that the slave instinct in woman is stronger because of her biological difference? When girls play with dolls, enjoying the role of little mother, or nurse, or homemaker, while the little boys are building bridges, or pushing toy trucks, does this tell us something of the difference in the sexes? Not necessarily. Many psychologists today believe that young children choose their playthings solely as a result of the cultural dictates. A little boy might be equally interested in dolls and trucks, until his parents or friends make it clear that "dolls are for girls, trucks are for boys."

In an attempt to recognize a sexual difference in handwriting we might use an old measuring rod and tentatively say that female reasoning is *subjective* while male reasoning is *objective*, though we know that each sex can reason both ways. We are, therefore, somewhat in the dark. In analyzing handwriting, then, it is important to know the sex of the writer, rather than to guess. Even an expert—although an attempted guess might be correct—could be mistaken.

In our present-day culture, women seem to have become more

masculine. Many people—especially men—have noticed this, and the graphologist sees more signs of independence and greater aggressiveness than a female writer's grandmother's handwriting disclosed. And our men appear to have become more "feminine," less independent and more intuitive. Whether we are moving toward a matriarchy or toward an equalizing of the sexes is a moot question which is under investigation by many social scientists.

The entire subject of why sex is not indicated in handwriting is one for serious speculation to the more than casual student of human nature, and I can only assert from my experience and observation that there are women who enjoy their slavish roles, while a large majority have had a taste of independence and like it. We find them swelling the ranks of the professions, political posts, the world of business, the arts and sciences. But it is my opinion that the woman who realizes herself as a wife, mother and homemaker, is still much happier in the final analysis than the one whose creations have added to the progress of the outside world, yet who is frustrated in her feminine role. An analysis of handwriting confirms this.

We seem to be confronted with two faces on the same coin: positive effects of woman's freedom and negative ones. And in the handwritings of ostensibly free women, we are bound to see conflict and must be careful how we evaluate it. The same freedom they sought and seem to have found makes it even more difficult for the graphologist to evaluate which sex component is stronger, the masculine or feminine. This makes it more necessary to reinforce the rule: *find out the sex of the writer before attempting to make an analysis of handwriting*.

The Writer's Age

Chronological age does not show in handwriting. What will be revealed are signs of maturity or a lack of it. None of us is entirely mature, although we keep striving to achieve maturity on various levels, and then develop only a measure of it. What is maturity? You may have your own definition, but it seems to me that it means the ability to accept the tedium of life, its responsibilities, and its "slings and arrows" philosophically.

We all know people of mature years who seem never to have grown up emotionally. A man or woman may be mature enough to assume responsibilities in relation to work, or family, or social relations, yet

17

be young in years. Others, old enough to know better, are still emotionally dependent, living in a past which once gave them what they construed as security they do not now feel they have. These people often shift responsibilities to others, and their handwritings reveal the extent of their dependence. Where we see evidence that someone has regressed to the infantile level, we are dealing with an emotionally sick person. On the other hand, handwriting may reveal that a subject is mature in the practical area and can make practical decisions, although we may also see indecisiveness and an emotional functioning on an infantile or adolescent level. Such handwritings show a capacity for making adjustments.

Take the hard-boiled business executive, for example. He is past middle age, has built up a thriving enterprise, and makes practical and astute decisions which involve huge sums of money. This same man, when his emotions become involved, might act like a little boy, expecting his wife, who represents the mother figure in his life and upon whom he is emotionally dependent, to make all the decisions regarding family life. His handwriting will reveal both strong and weak signs, and we have to be particularly careful how we balance one against the other in order to reach a correct conclusion.

Your own son of 14 may possess more poise and sense of responsibility than your husband at 45, who gambles his salary away every week at the race track while the boy works after school and brings every penny home. Line up their handwritings side by side and look for signs which tell the difference between them. There are many cases where the nominal head of a family is irresponsible and the burden falls upon the shoulders of one of the children. We hear such a boy (or girl) described as "old for his years."

Old age will usually be revealed in handwriting that is tremulous, with wavering strokes. It is not difficult to recognize. Yet it does not follow, all the time, that people of advanced years write such a hand. I know a woman past 80 whose handwriting shows enthusiasm and animation. Rising lines on the page indicate her optimism, and her t bars run far to the right of the stem of the letter. She is active, mentally alert, youthful in spirit and can set a good example to some of our young "beatniks" who are bored with life because they are so self-centered.

The nervous shaky handwriting should not be confused with the tremulous hand associated with old age. Such a writer may be suffering from shock to the nerves, as in the case of an excessive drinker, or he may have a tremor. Perhaps he was under great tension at the time the sample was written.

Some people write quickly and smoothly one day and so shakily the next day, or even a few hours later, that they cannot read their own scribbling. That is why it is always best, when attempting to analyze a handwriting, to be sure the person is in a relaxed, comfortable position, using a pen he chooses.

Try to find out your subject's age. In the case of a woman over 40, it might be tactful not to insist unless she volunteers the information. Many women will, and even cutting off a few years will not make much difference as long as you know in what age group your writer belongs.

A child's handwriting is usually easy to recognize because it is often a scrawl, done slowly. Frequently it slants downward because of the effort made when focusing attention on the letters and words. It is not wise to try to analyze the handwriting of a child under 12, unless you are an expert graphologist. (I have seen writing of boys and girls of this age which already revealed mental formations and may seem to have been written by an adult. Here there is intellectual maturity not in keeping with the physical and emotional development and I know I am dealing with a child who may be precocious or in the "problem" category.) A good rule to remember when you try to estimate maturity is: if the handwriting is very rounded, the person is childlike in many respects; where there is a great deal of angularity, this is a sign of development. But in any case, it is advisable to *know* the age of the writer.

Arguments For and Against

The common argument against graphology can be summed up in these words: "If I write a number of ways, how can you tell my real character?"

The answer is simple. A person who writes differently at different times is not only subject to changing moods but is also versatile. For instance: if your handwriting slants naturally to the right, it may take on a vertical angle when you are taking notes, since at such times you are not thinking spontaneously—you are taking down another person's thoughts. Or, your usual handwriting may be large or medium, and become very small when you are concentrating very hard on something.

If you are very tense, your letter formations may become cramped, even illegible, though normally your writing is readable and flowing. Although handwriting specimens may look different, the essential character will be revealed. Even if you write a number of different ways, the real you will emerge in all the specimens.

In 1792, J. Charles Grohman, professor of theology and philosophy, wrote a treatise in which he declared: "It is just as difficult to disguise one's handwriting as one's physiognomy." No one can disguise his or her handwriting consistently. Sooner or later, the real character shows through the disguise either in rhythm, letter forms, spacing, size of upper and lower loops, or punctuation.

One example of a disguised handwriting comes to mind. A man whose natural writing slanted to the right forged a number of checks. He had a habit of placing a period after his own name. (This is not a common habit.) The forged handwriting *looked* different, but each signature had a period after it, in the same position as that which he put after his own name. This was a sure giveaway.

In this man's many handwritings, I further observed similarities in rhythm, the height of i dots, t bars above the stem of the letters (a clue to his vivid imagination and reaching out for the unattainable). He had written the spurious checks to purchase something which was normally out of his financial reach. He lived in a world of fantasy; his entire life seemed to be a fiction he had invented. He described himself as a writer of stories about aviation and had stationery printed with the insignia of the Flying Corps. He limped, and explained this with a story about crashing in a plane. He lived in an expensive suite which he could not afford, but he obtained the money from some people who felt sorry for him because of his handicap, and from others who thought of him as a struggling writer with a great talent.

I was called into the case when he was apprehended for plagiarism, after copying, word for word, aviation stories by a well-known author. Since the forged checks were not the main issue, I (gratefully) did not have to testify against him.

He was sent to prison. While serving his term he wrote to me and I noticed that his handwriting took on a definite change. Instead of his natural right slant, it became vertical in angle—the same angle of the signatures on the disputed checks. The reason became obvious. Prison discipline forced him to become reflective and more realistic. His fundamental character—and he was a sensitive man with many admirable traits—remained the same.

In this instance, the prison environment had a positive effect. Released because of good conduct before his two-year term expired, he was determined to seek psychiatric aid. As his handwriting revealed to me, he had genuine literary ability. He later expressed himself through it as his psychoanalytic treatment began to help him.

In many handwritings of forgers I have observed, there is almost a total lack of character disclosed. It is as though their own characters are blanks, and they take on that of the person whose signature they are forging. The forger is usually artistic, which means he is strongly visual. What he does is draw the lines of the signature he is forging, and he does it so perfectly that this ultimately sounds his knell of doom. If he forges more than one document, the signatures are identical and the conclusion becomes obvious to the handwriting analyst. No one writes his signature exactly alike twice. The bank usually recognizes it even with its differences, although there are times when even the bank has doubts, as when a depositor is in a hurry, or in a nervous state, or signs a check while under the influence of alcohol. To the graphologist, however, the character of the writer becomes evident through major clues.

Getting back to the arguments against graphology, here is another: "If I disguise my handwriting, how can you tell which is my natural writing and which the disguise?" We suppose here that the examiner has the opportunity to see the natural writing, but in the absence of it there are still signs which give us clues to a disguised handwriting. A natural handwriting tends to flow easily if there are no neural disturbances.

Carefully observe the specimens on the next page. You will notice resemblances in all of them. The first, a disguise, is a backhand which shows the hiking up of words. The rhythm is slowed up, to be sure, but observe the letter forms, the t bars with hooks on them, the breaks between letters, and the final horizontal stroke in the last word, "price," which has the same hook as in the t bars. The Greek d appears in Specimens 1 and 2, as does the small printed s and the capital S. The tendency of the writer is to write a soaring hand because of her innate optimism, and you will see the upward swing of the basic lines—aside from the hiking up of words. Furthermore, the pen pressure is almost

DISGUISE

Ser what you can see and tell me
the truth — yes indeed, the truth at
any price —

SPECIMEN 1

NATURAL WRITING

See what you can see and
tell me the truth — yes indeed,
the truth at any price =

SPECIMEN 2

PRINTED DISGUISE

So you wont Think we are neglecting
you, we invite you to our party and
suggest you come early to avoid the
rush.

SPECIMEN 3

the same although in most instances pressure in a backhand becomes heavier as more emphasis is laid on disguising a hand. (The other reason is that the more the person swings away from *people* to write with a left slant, the more there is an interest in *things*, which is bound to result in heavier pen pressure.)

Now observe the natural writing with its easy flow and lack of tremulousness. (You may have to use a magnifying glass for this.) The spontaneous right slant tells us that the writer prefers to express herself impulsively; she is responsive, intuitive, intensely emotional. Innate talent is revealed in both these hands, with emphasis on artistic expression because of the strong intuitive faculty.

The printed specimen has to be examined even more carefully than the other two, for it is done deliberately. The circle i dots are an affectation (it often means this in any handwriting, for it expresses *artiness* when it doesn't appear in a handwriting showing a strong sense of design). However, letter formations still resemble those in the other two specimens. Again we observe the self-discipline in strong t bars. The small d is different in the printed disguise. The inverted writing usually means a strong masculine component in the writer. It must be admitted that this woman, although essentially feminine emotionally, has many of the elements of what we have come to consider a masculine mind. It was as natural for her to write this inverted formation as the Greek d. Finally, versatility is indicated in all three hands. There is also a sensuousness to forms, colors and music as shown in the rather heavy pen pressure, rhythm, consistent spacing (to make the samples *look* good). And the broad r in the printed sample is a clue to her visuality. The small capital S in the printed and backhand disguises tells us she was not as sure of herself as when she constructed a rather large one in her natural writing.

Some people argue that their handwriting cannot reveal their true character because it is not "natural" writing—they have deliberately copied someone else's writing because they admired it. Yet the real reason someone copies another person's handwriting is because he admires that person's traits. It is a way of trying to be like that person, and in itself reveals a lot about personality.

3. Neighbors

*Oh wad some power the giftie gie us
To see oursels as others see us!
It wad frae monie a blunder free us,
An' foolish notion.*
—ROBERT BURNS

Before delving into the fundamentals of handwriting, let's take a look at what graphology can reveal. As soon as you learn what to look for, you may want to experiment by analyzing the handwritings of your neighbors—if you don't live in a skyscraper! You may learn why one of them passes you by some mornings without greeting you and is effusive another time; why another is the noisy element in the house. If you have wondered why it took so long before you became acquainted with your next-door neighbor, a survey of his handwriting will tell you the reasons.

I tried this experiment once and the results follow. The young couple upstairs who left together each morning to go to their separate jobs were usually quiet and unobtrusive except when they gave an occasional cocktail party. Let's start with her handwriting (Textile Designer).

First we see that the handwriting *looks* different from the copybook style taught in school. She is, in fact, the product of a private school. A majority of girls from such educational institutions write in the same manner. The slant is vertical, showing an aloofness and reserve which go hand-in-hand with selectiveness. Some people consider her snobbish, and she is not lacking in this element. But the roundness of the writing indicates emotional pliability and receptiveness such as we find in children, and this means that she unbends when friendliness is extended to her.

I do want To say "Thank you" again r the most pleasant interview I had ith you yesterday. It was so nice

SPECIMEN 4

There are signs of sound practical judgment in the single downstroke of the y, where the final stroke is eliminated. The t bar above the letter shows imagination, while her carefully dotted i's tell us she has a retentive memory.

She told me she had just started working as an assistant to a textile designer. She is well suited for such work and will progress, since her handwriting reveals the combination of artistic talent and the practicality she needs to put it to a definite use.

Although friendly, she is not apt to permit a ready intimacy. The t bar which flies to the right of the stem in the words "want," "most," "pleasant" and "interview" shows enthusiasm. But she is self-contained and has poise, so that this enthusiasm would be expressed in her work rather than in her outward manner.

Her well-spaced lines and words express a fine sense of order and arrangement, and you would realize how true this is if you could see how neat, artistic and unusual her apartment is. She goes in for the modern in decoration and belongs, as well, to the modern school of thought insofar as she believes in independent self-expression. This is not the typically domestic or material woman for whom marriage as a career would be completely satisfactory. We conclude that she *is* different, and when she reaches the goal she has set for herself as a full-fledged designer, her designs will be different, too.

The designer's husband (Advertising Man) is more robust than the distaff member of the twosome. This is shown by heavy pen pressure which also reveals a sensuousness to forms, colors, music, line and structure. He has constructive ability as indicated in one form of the capital I he uses, as well as in the printed small s in the words "insight" and "since."

ADVERTISING MAN

January analysis. I that I have grown in insight since then,

SPECIMEN 5

His large writing coupled with wide spacing between the words tells us he likes to "spread himself," to do things on a lavish scale. In other words, he needs a large stage.

He is an advertising man who is acquainted with every angle of the business. His firmly crossed t bars tell us he has a strong will and is conscientious about performing a job in a balanced fashion. However, the t which ends in an upward stroke and has no bar, in the word "insight," gives us a clue to the kind of sensitivity which robs him of his initiative when it comes to starting something with which he is not familiar. (If this sign appears once in a brief specimen, chances are it would be repeated in a lengthier one.)

There is evidence of a retentive memory in the carefully dotted i's, and the first i in "insight" has a tent-like look that points to a keen critical faculty.

26

The slant of the writing is essentially vertical, although it sometimes veers to the right ever so slightly. This tells us that although he is reserved, his impulses sometimes overtake him and he expresses himself, at such times, with more spontaneity than usual.

The blunt endings or finals show obstinacy and the fact that he can be blunt, unyielding and "set" in some of his opinions. Notice how he forms his capital I two ways; this tells us he is versatile.

Although these two people are vastly different from each other in many respects, they have in common reserve and artistic interests and appreciation, and the very differences add stimulus to the relationship. He is the stronger of the two which is, perhaps, as it should be.

BANK ACCOUNTANT

In the banking business it is most im that a person have the ability to get along with people and to get along with people you mu understand them. It is my belief that a

SPECIMEN 6

This handwriting (Bank Accountant) is a bit of a puzzler, as are most that veer left in a backhand slant. The small writing coupled with the backward angle gives us a man who is essentially an introvert. He is, in fact, something of a hermit—the bachelor who lives alone and likes it!

There are a number of t bars which do not go through the stem of the letters, while others do. This means that although he is indecisive, lacking in self-confidence in some respects, he is nevertheless over-conscientious and capable of disciplining himself in his work.

The weak t bars which remain on the left side of the stem tell us also that he has never completely "grown up" emotionally, and that he lives in the past to some degree and is somewhat self-conscious.

Although he does not usually warm up to people, he has developed a friendly manner because of the demands of his position in the bank. He is passive and often starts things he does not finish, yet he is meticulous and has a desire for order, as is shown in his well-spaced lines and words. The small writing indicates powers of concentration. He should be well suited for a desk job where he doesn't have to mix with other people. He does well as an accountant, dealing with figures, but the same culprit, the weak t bar, tells us that he has never completely found himself and that he becomes restless and often feels frustrated.

The medium-light pen pressure tells us he is extremely sensitive. This is confirmed by the left slant of his writing, showing that he withdraws instead of making the effort to seek companionship which might expose him to hurts in human relationships.

Although this man is not emotionally integrated, he functions well in a bank. Because he is adjusted on the vocational level he finds a compensation for the frustrations which exist in the emotional area of his life. He has probably missed a great deal by remaining a bachelor, but he is not temperamentally constituted to talk much about himself. He is better as a listener.

MEDICAL STUDENT

she doesn't want him. But he's in

process of making life as comfortable a

himself while he writes a novel about

SPECIMEN 7

This girl of 19 (Medical Student) has wisely chosen the pursuit of medicine as a career. Intellectually, she is far above average, as can be seen in the mental formations of her h's where the loop is eliminated.

This is further corroborated by small writing showing powers of concentration. She is a natural student, with constructive ability as shown in the small printed s's in the words "she" and "himself." The fact that she makes an s two ways indicates versatility.

The literary g made to resemble a number 8 is a sign of adaptability, as well as a capacity for expressing herself in writing. It has other connotations, too: it belongs to a person who would always manage to see his (or her) way clearly no matter what the obstacles. (It is one of the cultural signs and often appears in conjunction with the Greek d and e.)

She possesses the ability to reason logically, as indicated in connected letters of the words "want him," "making," etc. There are also many breaks between letters—the sign of intuition. This means she has insight and observes more in a situation (or person) than may be evident in the externals. This gives us the clue to her potential as an excellent diagnostician, and if she so desires she could ultimately specialize (as indicated by her small writing). She has capacities to become a competent scientific researcher, too.

The spacing between lines and words is, perhaps, a little *too* wide and obvious, but it gives us, nevertheless, a clue to her desire for deliberation. This she carries to an extreme so that it places her on the neurotic borderline. We find this form of spacing in people possessing paranoid symptoms, although in this particular specimen the sign is mitigated by another sign—the spiritual one—in the bowed t bar which appears twice above the stem in the word "the." This tells us she has a capacity for self-discipline, control, a desire to overcome her weaknesses and to strive for betterment.

The pen pressure, although fairly light, has some dark strokes, telling us that she is sensitive but not always even-tempered. She recognizes this and is striving to overcome it by exercising self-control.

Her high i dots show imagination; those directly above the letter reveal her accurate memory.

Next (Aspiring Actress) is the impulsive, extroverted individual whose energies flow outward, as indicated in the rightward slant. She is warm, friendly, sensitive and imaginative, as shown in the t bar above the stem of the letter in the words "thinking," "the," "Northwestern." The final strokes rise upward many times, as in "am" and "drama," and tell us she is capable of being gracious and affable.

I am quite interested in drama and was thinking seriously of transfering to the Northwestern School of Speech

SPECIMEN 8

She is gregarious and social-minded, needs people and is anxious to make herself articulate in human relationships. She carries this desire into her goal of becoming an actress. While the writing does not express the emotional intensity of a Barrymore (since the pen pressure is more on the light side than heavy), it does indicate sincerity of feeling in its easy flow and roundness. We may conclude from this that she could achieve a measure of success on the stage in ingenue roles.

She seems unusually logical (factual) for someone whose emotions play a more important part than her reasoning in the forming of decisions. This is shown in connected letters with only one "intuitive" break in the long word "Northwestern." But this is probably because she lacks the experience which might develop her insight. However, even the one break gives us a clue to the fact that she has the capacity within herself for development. This may take a more expressive form after she has completed her studies and is on her own.

Struggling to get somewhere in the theatre should certainly develop inner resources. Yet she may decide to change her goal to a more practical one because of her factualness and lack of essentially artistic temperament.

However, because of evidence of imagination, she would be unhappy in routine work and should be engaged in some form of endeavor where her imagination would have opportunity for expression. She could find happiness in marriage.

(P.S. She did—since this book was started—and now has her second child. "Perhaps" she says, "some day my little girl will be an actress." An interesting commentary on how so many mothers realize their ambitions through their children!)

ARTIST

SPECIMEN 9

Here is the artist, accustomed to wielding a brush so that his pen marks often resemble brush strokes. There is rhythm in everything he does and he operates on a large scale.

He has intuition, as shown in many of the breaks which are so obvious in the words "with" and "will." But he can also reason logically, as indicated not only in connected letters but in the two connected words "of mine." (Joining words indicates a form of persistence often found in the handwritings of executives.)

We are dealing here with a man of many abilities. He is a prolific artist and his persistence is borne out in the long t bars which show his tremendous drive. The hook on the end of the t bar in the word "this" tells us he can hang on tenaciously to something he starts until it is finished. Thus, we have the inspired artist with a capacity for hard work which should add up to success. And the fact is that many of his illustrations have appeared in national magazines.

The right slant of the writing tells us he has a leaning toward people, is interested in them. They are the subjects of his paintings. He understands them fairly well, too, as his intuition coupled with judgment indicates.

31

When this specimen was written, he was considering a post as instructor in a leading art institute. During his residence in our apartment house, he used many of his neighbors as models for his illustrations and we all admired him, not only as a capable artist but as a real human being as well. He entertained lavishly (when he was not working), which would naturally be indicated by the largeness of his writing.

SCHOOLTEACHER

> *Good this time, and so want to be reasonably sure that t potentialities for a rewarde relationship exist with*

SPECIMEN 10

The writer of Specimen 10 was my next-door neighbor and I enjoyed a very pleasant relationship with her. She had formerly been a schoolteacher, and many of the signs associated with teachers of an earlier era exist in her handwriting. It is rounded, fairly uniform and slants to the right. This combination tells us she is friendly, warm, gentle. The light pen pressure is an indication of her sensitivity but it is the kind that is associated with consideration and concern regarding the feelings of others. (She was always careful not to intrude when she heard the tapping of my typewriter.)

There is a common-sense element in her nature, as shown in the connected letters revealing her logical reasoning. The single downstroke of the y's and g's, showing good judgment, confirms this.

The writing is well spaced between letters and words, telling us she is an orderly, well-organized person. Her tastes are simple and along conventional lines, although her desire for the cultural things shows in the g which is formed like number 8, even though it appears only once, in the word "good." There is nothing in the least bit aggressive about this individual. Rather, she is somewhat submissive, as shown in the t bars which are none too firm, even though they are centered on the stems. Since there is no intense emotional drive, the need for a strong will is not great. We are dealing here with a woman who is concerned with performing her duties and is submissive to the wishes of people stronger-willed than herself. She has a tremendous amount of patience, developed during her teaching days, which compensates for the lack of voltage behind her will.

Her husband (Specimen 11) is the dominant factor in the family group. Her 11-year-old daughter (Specimen 12) inherits the mother's warm, outgoing nature and some of the traits of her father.

SALESMAN

SPECIMEN 11

This (Salesman) is the husband of the former schoolteacher. He is the positive extrovert, the person whose energies flow outward and who is bent upon activity more than contemplation. A real estate broker, he is a salesman of better than average ability.

In the high t bars, many of them above the stem of the letter, we have an indication of a vivid imagination, a spirit of adventure, some of the elements of the perfectionist. The large writing indicates that he is guided more by emotional factors than by reasoning in his pursuits.

33

But he is no mental slouch, either, as shown in the angularity of formations indicating keenness, efficiency, resistance to obstacles. The fast rhythm of the specimen shows that he thinks quickly just as he does everything else, and that he has a great deal of energy, which is corroborated by many long t bars—the sign of driving power.

The involved capital H in "however" tells us he is a person who gets himself into complicated situations from which he can emerge through strategic moves.

However, there is a downward slant to the basic line and this indicates pessimism. In fairness to the writer, it must be said that this specimen was written at a time when he suffered a great financial loss which left him in a disheartened, pessimistic state.

Of the salesman and his wife, it is obvious that the husband is the domineering force, although the wife's patience and habit of "treading softly" are soothing antidotes to this high-powered individual. Because of his vivid imagination, he often anticipates the worst while she pours oil on troubled waters!

On the important levels, this couple is compatible. We might, however, observe his Heel of Achilles—forceful though he is—in the final stroke of the word "it." It is a leftward stroke which reveals acute sensitivity and, incidentally, a receptivity to that soothing syrup his wife hands out.

11-YEAR-OLD CHILD (MUSICIAN)

so I sat up all night writing it to hand in the next morning. My teacher was very complimentary when I ha

SPECIMEN 12

This is the 11-year-old daughter of the preceding couple. Although an obvious combination of both father and mother, she possesses apparent individuality. This shows in the formation of her capital M in the word "My," where the last mound is higher than the others. It is a clue to her drive for independence. (It means the same thing no matter what kind of hand it appears in.) She wants to be outstanding in whatever she undertakes. In this case (and for the time being), it is music.

She possesses a vivid imagination, as is shown in the consistent forming of t bars above the stem of the letter. The obviously rounded writing is typical of the child she is emotionally: pliable, responsive, not difficult to mold. There is also a consistent rhythm all through the writing and in the lower loops which gives us a clue to her instinctive musical responses. Her i dots are high when not directly above the letter, showing both her retentive memory and corroborating her imagination as revealed in the high t bars.

The initial and end strokes on the words "up," "to" and "was" tell us she is still following rules laid down for her in detail. But the good spacing between words and lines shows unusually well-organized planning abilities for a child of 11.

We conclude that she has a well-defined goal and is working toward it. The potentialities for success as a musician are evident (or she may decide later on to teach music). With the patient guidance of her mother and the enthusiastic encouragement of her doting father—for whom she has a great attachment—she has the necessary conditioning influences for success in later life.

The important thing to be observed here is that although we are dealing with an only child, she does not have the self-centered, isolated temperament of many children in this category. She retains a certain childishness without the precociousness often found in talented children, in spite of the element of independence.

Specimen 13 is part of a letter from another neighbor. The writer is a flyer, age 24. The t bar above the stem, in "thoughts" and "thoughtful," is the sign of the flyer. Often this formation appears in the handwritings of many dancers, writers, painters, or even people in ordinary walks of life who are perfectionists with a spirit of adventure and vivid imagination. It tells us the writer is reaching out for the unattainable (for the moon, so to speak). This t bar has a number of meanings. It indicates that the person making it has a rich fantasy life which is in keeping with a vivid imagination. But there are other signs here, too, which should be observed.

AVIATOR

As a younger person, m private thoughts - adventure - da of a thoughtful person .... the important to me. I have not changed. - the same addictions Perhaps too ... Same smile.

SPECIMEN 13

The small printed s which appears almost consistently all through the writing gives us an important clue to the youth's talent; it derives from his ability to discard the schoolroom forms he was taught and to build his own forms.

His imagination, intuition (shown in breaks between letters), and the mental formation of the small h where the initial stroke is eliminated, tell us that here is a person who can write. (He has written poetry; he can write fiction if he sets his mind to it.)

However, there are signs of struggle, of indecision, of the fact that he seems to be feeling his way. He is still in the process of growth. There is a sign of immaturity in the t bars which do not go through the stem of the letter. This is also the sign of restlessness, but through his insight (intuition) he is trying to come to terms with himself. The variety of t bars gives us the clue to a neurosis which, until he understands what caused it and learns to cope with it, may act as a stumbling block to the literary achievement of which he is capable. There is angularity in the shape of his writing, which reveals a measure of rigidity. This, together with the t bar which does not go through the stem of the letter, reveals the presence of tension. Even his capital I (a clue to his ego), unlooped at the top, seems to veer left and right, and tells us that he is not quite sure of what his identity should be. He has one sign which could bear explaining (described again further in the book) because it is one of the best, most hopeful signs in handwriting. It is the t bar which bows above the top of the stem, in the last word on the third line. It is a spiritual sign, but it is more. It shows a tendency to curb unruly impulses, to overcome weaknesses, to improve, to aim for betterment. Even if one such t bar appears in a handwriting which shows great emotional disturbance, it is a hopeful sign, revealing the overcoming of what the person considers bad in himself and the desire to replace it with good.

Further, his introspection and signs of introversion—causing him to enjoy flying solo in a plane at great heights where he feels detached from the world, and where his world of fantasy becomes the reality—show in the t cross which is on the left side of the stem and does not go through it. But there is a balance of practicality, an earthiness too. This is revealed in the letter d in the word "changed" which comes down in a blunt stroke at the end, indicating obstinacy, a tendency to be blunt in expression. And because the d is so spaced before the final stroke, we have the sign of a person who can be poker-faced and can remain stubbornly mute in some situations. (Watch the person with a poker face at a game of cards, then examine his handwriting, if possible, and see if it doesn't show this kind of a small d.)

4. Fundamentals in Handwriting

It is the handwriting itself that is important to the graphologist, never *what* is written. Do not consider the text of the specimen, as it may mislead you. The writer may not mean what he is saying, or he may be quoting someone to leave an impression. Although there are instances when the text is helpful, the expert graphologist is not interested in it, but sees only the handwriting.

Since there are so many details to consider when analyzing a handwriting, it is best to systematize your approach. These are the fundamentals to be concerned with.

Pen Pressure—The pressure relates to the senses and to some extent reveals the vitality of the individual. It will be heavy, medium-heavy, "muddy," medium-light, light, or extremely light so that it appears hair-like. (Muddy pressure must not be confused with shaded writing; it is usually unpleasant to the eye while shaded writing often looks artistic.) Observe the writer's vitality—is he robust, athletic, delicate, supersensitive, unhealthy? If he is "out of this world" it will be indicated by extremely light writing, "spiritual" lack of pen pressure, corroborated by other signs in the handwriting.

Slant—As Dr. Alfred Adler, the famous Viennese psychologist, said: "Handwriting points the way from me to you." It follows that the *slant* of an individual's handwriting will express whether his way is one of ardor, affection, reserve or withdrawal. There is the extreme rightward-flowing handwriting; the moderate right angle; the vertical, moderate backhand; and the extreme left-slanted backhand. In the slant (or slope) you discover whether the person is outgoing, extroverted, leaning toward people; or the opposite, which is reserved, introverted, unsocial or even antisocial. These are general categories, since more than the slant has to be considered in estimating the extent of extroversion and introversion in individuals.

Size—The size of the writing gives us clues to the individual's manner of approaching a situation. Does he generalize or observe details? The size really represents the kind of lens through which a person sees. Is it unusually large, large, medium-large? (All three sizes give a clue to a degree of exhibitionism.) Or is it "normal," which does not particularly strike the eye? This is the size most people write. The smaller the writing, the better the powers of concentration. Microscopic writing belongs to the specialist, the hermit, the introvert (no matter what the angle). The lens of the eye sees everything in minute detail as through a microscope.

Basic Line—Whether the lines run uphill, downhill or in both directions relates to the writer's point of view and his spirits. Is he optimistic, buoyant, cheerful, euphoric? Or skeptical, depressed, temporarily unhappy, suffering from melancholia, suicidal? Sometimes lines veer upward but words hang down either in the middle of a sentence or at the end of many sentences. You may see temporary or chronic depression, morbidity, hopelessness in these signs. The downhill writer is often the skeptic whose attitude arises from self-doubt. Here the basic line must be considered in conjunction with the t bars. Downhill writing is often a warning of depleted vitality, forerunner to a breakdown. Estimate very carefully.

Margins and Spacing—The width or narrowness of margins and spacing between words determine the width or narrowness of a person's mind, his aesthetic reactions, whether he is a clear or muddled thinker, whether he is economical or extravagant. There may be wide spacing between letters in words, between the words, or between the lines. Or there may be no appreciable space between any of these. Perhaps there is a large margin on the right, on both right and left, or a margin that starts narrow and widens as the writer fills the page. The opposite may occur, where the margin starts wide and narrows as the page is filled. If the writing is poorly spaced in every respect so that it *looks* disturbed, you are probably dealing with a mentally and emotionally disturbed person. It will also be inconsistent in slant and pen pressure, and will have varying t bars and overly high upper loops. (Don't try to analyze it unless you are an expert. It might be the handwriting of a person who needs hospitalization, and you may have suspected it.)

t Bars—They are extremely important in determining how much will power, drive, energy, determination (or a lack of these) the writer has and how much he uses. The t bars reveal whether he is aggressive, persistent, compulsive; or weak, timid, vacillating, indecisive, passive, neurotic. In the t bar you will see clues to emotional immaturity; to whether the writer lives in the past or drives his energy ambitiously toward the future. Many handwritings will show a variety of t bars, all of which have special meanings. The t bar, together with other horizontal strokes, shows the extent of the writer's balance—how he copes with life's situations. The vertical strokes are indicative of elemental forces and how much influence they have in his life. They also give us clues to sexual energy.

i Dots—The i dots, considered in combination with the t bars and other letter formations, show, among other things, retentiveness or lack of it, imagination, humor and critical faculties. Are the dots high, close to the letter, wavy, pointed, circled?

Small Letters (the abc's)—Observe these in conjunction with other signs. Are they printed, copybook style, open or closed, angular or rounded or both? They indicate conformity to rules, mental development, caution, generosity and other personality traits.

Capitals—The capital letters denote taste and pride. Are they ornate, simple, printed, old-fashioned, artistic, open at the top or closed tightly with a loop? Do they start with an incurve or an outgoing flourish; are they rounded or angular? Do capital letters appear where small ones would normally be?

Loops—Upper and lower loops have a special significance. Notice whether they are wide, narrow, compressed, ragged at the top, very high; whether the lower ones are exaggerated and run into the line below. Are they the outstanding feature in the entire handwriting? Do they have a "broken back" look? Or is there, instead of loops, a single stroke—the uppers in the letters l, h, k, the lower ones in y's and g's? Breaks in loops, both upper and lower, reveal the presence of a physical impairment.

Zones—Divide the writing into three zones: upper, middle, and lower. The upper zone (loops especially) symbolizes the person's ideals, fantasy life, set of principles, standards; the middle zone concerns his approach to reality, how he deals with practical problems; the lower zone gives us clues to his physical demands, sexual potency, primitive impulses, materiality. Balance the three zones, as you would a mathematical problem. They will give you clues to more about the person than meets the eye.

Initials and Terminals—Initial strokes, often unnecessary, show attention to detail. The terminals, too, give valuable clues. Are they long, wavy, curving upward or downward, abrupt, blunt, or do letters end with a long horizontal line that has a hook on it? The terminals (or finals) are clues to how much *give* the person has. Does he give of himself? Of his material possessions? Is he loquacious, generous, curious, possessive? Or sensitive, touchy, simpering, sadistic, outgoing or introverted? Does he have more "won't" power than will power? Taken in conjunction with other signs and strokes, terminals give us important clues to many traits of character.

Speed (rhythm)—Indicative of energy, it tells you how much the person expends in the way he does things as well as how he thinks— whether slowly or quickly. The person who thinks more quickly than his hand can record may leave out some letters in words or slur a word ending in *ing*. He writes as though recording his thoughts in shorthand. There are two kinds of speedy writing— distinct and indistinct. The distinct writer slows down his thinking in order to conform; the indistinct writer can't bother with conforming but goes ahead and expresses himself, later rearranging his thinking to make it fall into a comprehensible pattern. The slow thinker appears to draw every letter and the speed, therefore, is slowed down. He is also careful of punctuation, unless he is illiterate or negligent. *Uneven* speed produces letters lacking in uniformity and may be corroborated by other signs of disturbance in the writing. Writing that is too speedy shows anxiety, which is further revealed in a going over or patching up of letters or words. Words crossed out in a messy looking specimen tell us the person is in an emotional mess. Writing in anger will show uneven pen pressure, blunt downstrokes, thick t bars, and the speed will be evident if you try to imitate the writing. When you have learned to estimate the speed of a person's writing you will know something about his energy output: whether he is lazy, indolent, indecisive because of tension, or, at the other extreme, whether he is a human dynamo.

Connecting Strokes—A word is either connected in its letter forms or it is broken up. When the entire writing is connected, with even words joined together, consecutive reasoning or logic is revealed. The person may also be literal-minded. If breaks appear, this is the sign of intuition. Where the handwriting is entirely broken up, looking like printing but not printing, it is the "inspirational hand." Many poets, artists, and dancers print consistently. So do engineers. Connected writing combined with breaks in some words shows that the writer is capable of logic, yet possesses some intuition.

Legibility—While the legibility of the writing gives no real clue to the writer's mentality, it does indicate whether he has a desire to communicate his thoughts. Or does he seem to have something to hide?

Punctuation—Careful punctuation indicates the writer's attention to details. Such care may be evident in the writing of an intelligent person. However, the person concerned with larger issues, with essences rather than details, may be careless in both punctuation and spelling, yet have a high intelligence rating. It is wise, therefore, to withhold judgment until the handwriting has been categorized according to which intellectual group the person belongs in. The meticulous person whose punctuation is flawless may also be a rigid, unimaginative one. One sure conclusion we can draw from the person who punctuates carefully is that he is obedient to the rules taught and often follows them to the letter. Careless punctuation, on the other hand, often shows a person who makes his own rules and can't be bothered with details, especially if someone else demands they be followed. Where there are dashes, these often serve as a period, but they show, nevertheless, either a kind of mental twist or a desire to be original or different. (In graphology, the *intent* is considered more important than the form used to express the thought.) Any departure from established rules of writing tends to show the state of the mind at the time it was concentrated on the act of transferring thoughts to paper.

Underscoring (other than signatures)—This means a form of capriciousness, may mean delicacy of thought, but always indicates *emphasis*.

Where there is too much underscoring under words, we are confronted with a type of emphasis which points to fanaticism. Who has not seen the religious fanatic's chalk writing on sidewalks or fences, underscored many times, quoting passages from the Bible?

Signatures—The way a person signs his name gives an important clue to his personality. It is the face shown to the outside world, the façade that is presented, and it may be at variance with the *real* person. The signature may be entirely different from the rest of a person's writing, or it may be harmonious with it. People in the public eye often underscore their signatures. If a writer does this and is not a public figure, he either hopes some day to be or wishes to be noticed wherever he is. The underscored signature has the psychological connotation of an inferiority complex compensated by personality force. A signature that is involved and indecipherable tells us that the individual writing it wishes to be enigmatic, and makes no attempt to achieve a clear line of communication with the other fellow. The simple, legible signature tells us the person has no desire to hide anything, but wants to achieve clear communication with others.

The next chapters will discuss each of these fundamentals in detail.

REMEMBER THIS RULE

A sign occasionally shown indicates an occasional trait.

When plentiful, it shows a habit.

When scarce yet evident, it reveals a tendency.

Even a sign that appears *once* in an entire handwriting is a clue to something that might develop under certain circumstances. For example, in the handwriting specimen of the aviator on page 36, the spiritual sign appears in the bowed t bar above the stem of the letter. This shows there is a striving for something better. If you see this sign in a person who is emotionally sick, depraved, degenerate or antisocial, no matter how low he has sunk on the moral scale, there is hope for him.

5. Pen Pressure

It is important to consider the type of pen a person chooses because it gives the analyst a clue to the kind of pen pressure he produces. He may be using a pen entirely unsuited to his kind of pen pressure. If a person who prefers a stub pen writes with a fine point, the pen may even go through the paper. The choice of a stub pen already tells us that his pen pressure is heavy or medium-heavy, and we know he belongs in the fundamental or materialistic category.

Heavy Pressure

We say the person who writes with heavy pressure is materialistic, but the word does not necessarily imply that he is grasping or money-mad. It merely means that his interest is primarily in concrete reality—in things he can see, hear, feel and taste. Every handwriting will have corroborating signs to tell you whether the person being analyzed is essentially materialistic or just partly so.

Heavy-pressure writers are usually physically robust, so that there is a positive voltage behind their pens as they write. They are, for the most part, the outdoor individuals—men and women who are interested in athletics. Among these writers, too, are businessmen who are primarily interested in the material results of their efforts. Other people take second place in their consideration. There is a strong element of the primitive in them, and they have healthy appetites, a strong sensuousness to forms, colors and odors—to everything that appeals to the senses. The man who prefers his boat or car to the company of other people belongs in this category. An inanimate thing becomes his love-object, and a woman may be looked upon as a possession. A majority of these heavy-pressure writers are adventurers by instinct. They are often intensely emotional, impulsive, concerned much more with activity than with spending time in contemplation. They are the doers, often the pioneers. Many of them enjoy working with their hands.

*the check, for you
Life is quite a*

SPECIMEN 14

Specimen 14 belongs to an artist whose first interest is his work. He prefers to use a heavy pen, or even a brush because it allows him to write comfortably. The primitive element is here diluted by a cultural background, giving him the veneer of civilization, but underneath there remains the robust, sensuous, adventurous human being. With him art comes first and people are his secondary interest. They are grist for his artistic mill.

Medium-Heavy Pressure

We encounter medium-heavy pressure in the writing of people from every walk of life: surgeon, artist, craftsman, butcher, mechanic, stevedore and unskilled worker. Here the interest is often divided between things and people. Where we recognize this, another type comes into being. Because I believe it is normal to be interested in both *things*, for physical comfort, and *people* to fill our social life, I have named this type the *Normal*. Specimen 15 is an example.

*marrying. Will you please
tell me whether or not you
think that we have an*

SPECIMEN 15

Here the roundness gives us a clue to a pliable nature which is affectionate (as shown in the slant), while the pen pressure, although seemingly heavy, produces a form of shading. (It may not be easy for the amateur to recognize the fine differences in the beginning, but after a while the eye will become accustomed to discerning them.) If you don't grasp exactly what I mean by "shading," look at the specimen under a magnifying glass. (You should have one, anyhow. It helps a lot.) Actually, the writer was using a pen which was too heavy for the pressure, as the ink flowed too readily from it and filled in the upper loops.

Light Pressure

The individual who chooses a pen with a fine point already tells us that he is extremely sensitive. He produces writing that is very light and delicate. His approach to life is not as heavy-footed as that of the heavy-pressure writer.

In Specimen 16, the pen pressure is fairly light, even though some strokes are heavier. There is sensitivity here, but there is also a slight element of robustness. The interest is primarily in people, indicated by the strong slant to the right.

SPECIMEN 16

Specimens 17 and 18 are of the light variety, although the slant of each is different. Nevertheless, the delicate pen pressure has the same meaning for both. The writer with the right slant shows a greater need for people and more acute sensitivity to what others think of him. The person who writes vertically shows unusual sensitivity, but the angle indicates that he can be more self-sufficient and is not as affected by what other people think of him. He has more reserve.

46

much if you can give me
more information on the
subject and how much.

SPECIMEN 17

to know just where the
hospital is located & what

SPECIMEN 18

Changes in Pressure

When there is a sharp change in pen pressure, we are often dealing with a person who is emotionally unstable. He may go along on an even keel for a while and then suddenly, without warning, show signs of temper or fury. Wherever the pen pressure is uneven, the person presents some kind of an emotional problem. Especially is this true of what may be called muddy (or pasty) pressure, as in Specimen 19. Because the angle here is vertical (indicating the writer's ability to check impulses and to withdraw into himself), we are not certain what he may be thinking since he appears self-contained. We say about him that his handwriting reveals instability, moderately controlled.

e have no permanent home as
et but we're optimestic and ex-
ect to get our own little place i

SPECIMEN 19

Where there seems to be no real pressure on the pen, as in Specimen 20, we are dealing with an unhealthy person. It is an obvious lack of vitality that prevents the writer from leaning heavily on the pen. In this case, the illness is both physical and emotional, and it is hard to tell which came first.

he or she can keep the

patients confidence —

if he has passed

SPECIMEN 20

Where pen pressure is light or medium-light and suddenly becomes heavy, as if the person were showing sudden emotional intensity or getting furious, we look for signs of temper. If the handwriting shows self-control, the very sign which manifests this, the t bar, may also reveal the presence of temper. For example, anger, resentment or bitterness may appear in a club-like ending of the t bar. It will also show in other strokes throughout the specimen of writing. In Specimen 21 we have a good example of a controlled person in whom there is much fury.

We have two Sons, animy on

and half after we married —

SPECIMEN 21

The slant, pen pressure and outstanding sudden dark strokes all corroborate each other. It is important to consider the size of the writing, too, as explained in Chapter 7.

48

6. Slant

"Handwriting points the way from me to you."—Dr. Alfred Adler

The *slant* of the handwriting, whether it is to the right, vertical (straight up and down), or to the left (backhand), will express the writer's approach to other people. It will reveal whether he is affectionate and demonstrative, reserved and self-contained, or aloof, undemonstrative, impersonal. It will fall into one of these three main areas, although the *degree* expressed may be determined by the degree of the slant. Other terms for the slant are the angle of inclination and slope.

A person may be able to write with ease in two angles, to the right and vertically. This shows versatility. He may be informal and act spontaneously with intimate friends, yet be formal and aloof with strangers. If the natural slant is to the right, he may write vertically when copying something or taking a message over the telephone. This is one reason why it is best to examine a specimen which has been written spontaneously, not copied.

Right Slant

These are the social, gregarious, affectionate and demonstrative individuals in whom the need for other people determines their greatest interest. They choose the kind of vocation in which they are in contact with other people; human relationships are more important to them than material gain. They are the extroverts whose energies flow outward, and they are usually more bent upon activity than contemplation. They are the sentimentalists whose emotions, more than reasoning, guide them in the forming of important decisions.

In this group we find the salesman, actor, teacher, politician, social worker, physician, nurse, and so forth. (There are exceptions to this rule, of course, for introverts exist in these categories, although it is often discovered that their occupations were not of their own choosing.) However, the majority of these people are "joiners" and comprise the large number who make up the social structure of society.

The interest in people has its origin in family conditioning. When there are a number of children in a family, the social instinct is more strongly developed. The only child seldom falls into this category, for he is brought up in a relatively isolated state. (There are exceptions to this, too, as indicated by the 11-year-old girl in "Neighbors.")

The diagram below corresponds to the varying slants that appear in handwriting. The left side represents the backhand writers who show different degrees of introversion; the right side represents the rightward-slanting hand of extroverts; "X," in the center, belongs to the vertical writer.

EMOTIONAL BAROMETER

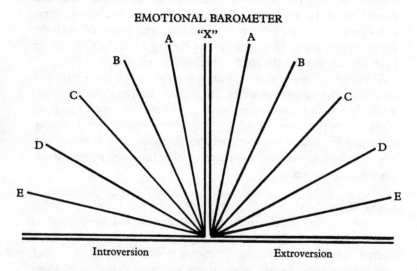

On the right side of this "Emotional Barometer" A and B belong to individuals writing at a *moderate* right slant. A is closer to "X" and is more reserved than B, and there is a tendency to write vertically when in certain moods. Specimens 22 and 23 correspond to A and B. They are the handwritings of individuals who moderately show what they feel.

Enclosed handwriting as well

SPECIMEN 22 (A on the barometer)

*t. In view of my own opinion, I
interested to read what you will*

SPECIMEN 23 (B on the barometer)

The writers of Specimens 24 and 25 are more demonstrative. Notice the greater angle of the slant.

*Graphology but have had grea
in obtaining any looks on the*

SPECIMEN 24 (C on the barometer)

*can t afford to m
Your advice will aid me*

SPECIMEN 25 (D on the barometer)

Specimen 26 is in a class by itself. The writer is capable of very intense emotion. The extreme right slant reveals extreme ardor.

SPECIMEN 26   (E on the barometer)

Where the writing leans extremely far to the right, we are confronted with a form of outer expression that often approaches hysteria. Such a writer cannot function adequately without other people. He usually marries young. If the mate dies, there is an unbridled demonstration of grief, but since this permits the emotions complete release, it is not long before the person again feels the need for intimate companionship, and therefore marries again. The opposite is true of the person who writes with an extreme backward slant. He also is intensely emotional, but he is withdrawn, detached and undemonstrative. In a similar bereavement, this person does not show the grief which is just as deeply felt, and it is doubtful whether he or she would ever marry again.

If you try to imitate either an extreme right slant or backhand, you will notice that the more extreme the angle, the heavier the pen pressure.

Vertical Writing

This is the angle of *reserve*. The writer is usually self-contained, calm, somewhat aloof. Emotions may be intense but they are held in check by the mind which sits in judgment over the impulses. Most vertical writers have a certain charm which is the result of poise and good manners. They are often friendly in their manner but do not permit a ready intimacy on the part of others.

In vertical writing which is small and possesses mental formations (explained in Chapter 12), there is a prevalence of reason over emotion most of the time.

Most vertical writers are realists, and although sentiment may not be lacking in their nature, they often deliberately avoid showing it. They are usually selective in their choice of friends, and many so-called "snobs" fall into this category. There may be an equal share of extroversion and introversion in a person writing a vertical hand, depending upon the type of work he does. For instance, an actress's writing may be vertical and large, indicating a preponderance of extroversion, while a research worker's will be small, accenting the introversion. Very large writing in any slant indicates a good share of extroversion. The fullness of expression it shows tells us the person is making a bid for attention.

Then there is the typical vertical hand of the product of a private school. Not in vain has it been said that many of them turn out snobs, for there is in some types of vertical writing something of a better-than-thou attitude.

Consider now a variety of examples written in a vertical angle. In Specimen 27 there is a large share of extroversion despite the angle because the writing is large and spread out.

SPECIMEN 27

Specimen 28 is the intellectual (mental type) whose small, vertical writing is well formed. It shows the Greek d and literary g made like number 8.

SPECIMEN 28

Specimen 29 is the artistic type, indicated by unusual letter forms and shaded pen pressure.

SPECIMEN 29

Specimen 30 is the typical snob, the perfect hostess with a superior attitude toward those who are not in her social realm or who don't have a "family tree." We see this in the vertical angle, angular formations, and the t bar which flies upward, indicating the social climber in this kind of hand. Notice also that the writing looks as though it were done with the aid of a ruler. The writer does everything with precision and formality.

SPECIMEN 30

Left Slant

There are fewer people who write backhand than there are right-slanters. On this side of the barometer, we find the people who are repressed, aloof, inhibited, and less interested in people than in things. A very small backhand indicates an interest in abstractions.

Although a backhand writer may appear communicative and friendly and may mix with other people, it is in a detached and impersonal way. There is always some kind of a barrier between him and others. Actually, such a writer prefers the society of the "choice few" with whom he identifies. And even those close to him, through family ties or marriage, have difficulty reaching him. Not without reason has the backhand been referred to, graphologically, as the "joker" in the pack of cards. Few people are able to evaluate accurately the writer of this angle, for he keeps himself barricaded, usually because of experiences of isolation in childhood which set him apart from others.

Sometimes, in such a writer, the inhibiting factor becomes anesthetized by some external stimulus—perhaps alcohol, or a shock of some kind. Then his reserve is apt to be temporarily abandoned and he may reveal glimpses of his real self.

Women who write backhand frequently have a strong masculine component. They lack the submissiveness of the spontaneous rightward-slanting writer. Such women often appear elusive and something of a mystery and they may go in for adventurous episodes. Often, too, they appear cold, deliberate, impersonal. They are concerned much more with a world of material things than with people. They may use people as a means toward achieving their goals.

It is not unusual for a young girl who writes backhand to marry a man very much older. The influences that conditioned her may have insulated her against the harsh effects of the outside world—thus her choice of a father figure. If her elderly husband treats her as a prized possession and places her in luxurious surroundings, she is usually satisfied, and she uses him to protect herself from the world. She is often selfish, self-indulgent, sexually frigid—and therefore happiest in a world of *things*.

It takes a long time for the backhand writer to warm up to others. Yet once the attachment is formed, it is lasting. It would be hazardous for a person whose handwriting falls on the extreme right of the "emotional barometer" to marry someone on the extreme left. They could never really get together, as the distance between their temperaments is too great to gap.

A child who feels rejected often develops a backhand, abandoning the method he is taught in school. Therefore a backhand tells us that the writer may have led an isolated life either as an only child or as a member of a family in which he felt rejected. As a result, he rebelled against a world in which he felt he did not belong and withdrew into a fantasy world of his own.

If you select the backhands from among the handwritings of a group of students, you will find that they were written by the students who seldom enter into group activities. They are usually the timid, retiring ones who hang back while the right-slanters forge ahead. Their fellow students may consider them snobs because of their aloofness, yet often it is merely a painful self-consciousness that prevents them from mixing with the others. They are, in fact, much more sensitive than their extroverted classmates who more readily overcome their self-consciousness as they learn to mix with other people.

You may hear someone say, "I developed a backhand because someone I knew wrote that way and I liked the looks of it. It's not my natural writing at all." That is only superficial reasoning. The real reason such a person emulated another's handwriting is because he admired that individual's traits. In emulating the handwriting, it was his way of showing that he wanted to be like that person.

The following examples are of different degrees of left slant or backhand. Specimen 31 belongs to a product of a private school. Some flexibility in the nature is seen in the roundness, in the way the small m's and n's are formed.

to be realistic about the future, however, and I very much fear that his

SPECIMEN 31 (Close to "X" on the barometer)

56

The next two examples of backhand differ in the pen pressure and form. Specimen 32 is slightly more to the left and rounded; Specimen 33 is angular.

SPECIMEN 32 (A on the barometer)

SPECIMEN 33 (B on the barometer)

The pressure in Specimen 34 is quite heavy. The writer is extremely emotional—but no one would know it for he is detached and undemonstrative.

SPECIMEN 34 (C on the barometer)

Not many people write with an extreme backhand. Try to imitate it and see how difficult it is, unless your own handwriting veers to the left.

Something should be said here about the "southpaw," the person who writes with his left hand. Peculiarly enough, very few left-handed people write backhand, although it would seem more natural that they should. It is safe to assume that there is some introversion in the southpaw even when his writing flows to the right. Where adjustments have been made—and there is always a need for a person writing with his left hand to make adjustments in a right-handed world—the t bars will be firm for the most part, although there are bound to be some which do not go through the stem of the letter. Such t bars may be interpreted as belonging to a person who has made some adjustments, although he still has more to make.

Several Slants

There is also the handwriting which reveals a variety of angles—to the right, vertical, left-slant. We may accurately conclude that the person is yanked in many directions. Sometimes he is outgoing and spontaneous, at other times withdrawn, self-contained and reflective. Occasionally he may withdraw completely, as though retreating into his shell. Often such a person is mercurial, unstable, unpredictable, difficult to pin down. He may be severely controlled in one area—some strong, bowed t bars will show this—but the varying angles tell us there are forces within him pulling one against the other, and we

VARYING ANGLES AND t BARS

SPECIMEN 35

must look for the signs of neurosis. No one can be so changeable without suffering anxiety and depression, although there might also be signs of euphoria, where some of the lines soar on the page as though the lift the person feels takes him up into his world of fantasy.

Signs of instability will show not only in the variety of angles, but in the t bars, too. Some may be forceful with a hook on the end; others weak and not going through the stem of the letter; a few may even slant downward, showing the sign of the rebel. Specimen 35 is a fair example.

7. Size

The size of a person's handwriting will tell a great deal about how he sees the world around him. It might be compared to the type of lens he uses to make his observations.

Large writing belongs to the person who sees the picture of anything—a plan, a person, a thing—in its entirety first; in other words, he gets a general view.

Small writing tells us that the person sees everything as though through a microscope, in minute detail.

Very large writing of any slant or formation will always disclose the person who wants to be noticed, the exhibitionist. It indicates at the same time a certain form of extravagance. The person may be extravagant with himself, or he may be lavish with others. Which it is will be determined by letter formations. However, you can always be sure that a person writing a large hand prefers to do things on a grand scale.

There are people who can write with equal ease in both a large and small hand. These are the versatile ones who can spend some time concentrating on details but are also able to get into action. They may first generalize about a situation, then break it down and observe the component parts that make up the general picture.

Abnormally large writing will give a clue to some abnormality in the writer. We might compare it to a photograph that has been enlarged so much that the figures in the picture are distorted. In every instance extremely large writing shows some exaggeration in the writer's viewpoint, or excessiveness in one direction or another.

Specimen 36 is an example of large, clear writing, executed with firmness in an upright (vertical) hand. Because this is the angle of aloofness, we are certain that the writer is extravagant with herself and has an exaggerated opinion of herself. (You have probably seen her photograph on the society pages of newspapers many times.)

SPECIMEN 36

Look at the next two examples of large writing, Specimens 37 and 38. Each is of a different type, yet both writers have in common an inability to concentrate on one thing for any length of time. Specimen 37 shows an outgoing quality while 38 reveals more reserve.

SPECIMEN 37

SPECIMEN 38

The majority of people write in what might be called a medium-large hand. Examine a fairly large collection of handwritings of people in different walks of life and this will soon become evident. The extremely large ones and microscopically small ones will belong to those individuals who are unusual in one way or another. You might even have difficulty reading the very small writing without a magnifying glass; you would probably have as much puzzlement understanding the machinations of a mind that produces it.

Usually, the very small hand belongs to the introvert. This means that most of the person's energy is generated into thinking rather than doing. However, where a small hand also shows signs of determination in long t bars, it indicates a person who does get into action after concentrating for a long time. Specimen 39 is a good example of this.

SPECIMEN 39

The traits of the hermit are also rather strong in writers of a small hand. They often prefer to live alone in isolated areas, cultivating only a few friends with whom they seldom, if ever, become intimate. For the most part, they are selfish, and they observe human beings as a scientist examines microbes under a microscope. They are usually theorists. In Specimen 39, again, there is a mixture: the capacity for theorizing or planning something in minute detail and then getting into action.

The writer of Specimen 40 also combines these elements, but here there is more pliability and gentleness. This is shown by the roundness of the letter forms. (The broken-back upper loops have an unhealthy connotation, explained in Chapter 14.) This is the writing of a hermit with strong powers of concentration.

SPECIMEN 40

Where there is a lack of uniformity in letters, some of them large and others small, we conclude that the writer observes life with some inconsistency. He may see situations in detail at one time and generalize at other times. We describe him as having an undisciplined mind, especially where the writing shows weak t bars. Specimen 41 is an example of an extreme case of this kind. The writing *looks* disturbed and we are safe in assuming that the writer is mentally aberrated.

SPECIMEN 41

Then there is a form of inconsistency in small writing where *one* feature in it is outstanding, as in Specimen 42. This may be, and often is, in long lower loops which run into the line below. It gives us a clue to an obsession in the nature of the writer, and the same meaning holds true in any kind of handwriting. In this very small writing it emphasizes an obsession with money, and it is also tied up with an exaggerated sexual drive. We might describe this person as a hermit who imagines himself a great lover in his fantasy, and who may readily work off his sexual energy in athletic activities.

SPECIMEN 42

The size of the writing in Specimen 43 indicates that the writer is a fairly normal person. It is neither small nor large; it might be considered a medium-large hand. The writer's interest is primarily in people (note the slant). We find the large majority of people in this category. Of course other features of handwriting must be considered before we can reach definitive conclusions about individual character.

has always come easy to
cherish it more as a soci
zy than as a serious

SPECIMEN 43

8. Basic Line

Time cools, time clarifies; no mood can be maintained quite unaltered through the course of hours.—THOMAS MANN

From the way the lines ascend or descend on the paper we get clues to the writer's disposition. Is he optimistic, cheerful, buoyant; on a fairly even keel; pessimistic and negative; depressed, melancholy, suicidal? Does he have intense mood swings? Is there the resilience to swing back to reality and continue to function, or do his moods influence him so much that his energy is tied up in a neurosis?

Rising lines seem to be dictated by an upsurge of energy, and the person says he's "happy." Even when a mood of depression seems to dominate the feelings for a short time, if the lines rise on the page we can be sure the writer is bolstered by hopefulness.

Handwritings of suicides have convinced me that it is usually the optimist who takes his own life. Picture him consumed with enthusiastic fervor which reaches great heights, taking him into a rich world of fantasy, and then being catapulted back into the world of reality with a painful shock. Since reality is never as glowing as the fantasy built up, disillusion is inevitable. Imagine the terrific let-down! Hopelessness replaces optimism, and in its throes comes a feeling of futility. If the depression is strong enough to heat up the brain to irrationality, the result is a desire for self-destruction.

However, this is an extreme case and not to be confused with the optimistic, cheerful, hopeful person who prefers, no matter what happens, to look on the bright side of life.

In the following samples we see first the optimist (Specimen 44); then the person who is usually on an even keel, coming to terms with his moods and dealing with them in a mature way (Specimen 45). Some words may tend to slant downward, but here the strong t bar tells us there is balance and self-control.

'll also no...
befos she can be just
uch less ideal. I would
much to see you and talk
have phoned seneral times
with no luck but if you do
not wish to see me — that
is my misfortune.

SPECIMEN 44

However, such was not the
a frontal lobotomy case.
operation, she was terribly

SPECIMEN 45

We often see the unhappy, worried individual who finds life a burden. He says he is happy but his handwriting refutes it. The truth is, he is a contradiction in terms, for he is happiest when most unhappy! Do you know such a person? If so, look at his handwriting and ponder.

Many of us may be temporarily unhappy because of a loss of a loved one or some crisis in our lives, even though we are generally optimistic. This will show in rising lines at the beginning of a document (a letter, note, notations in a diary), while toward the end of the lines, the last word often will fall down or over. Many times the entire line veers downward. Such persons may have suicidal thoughts and may even, in a moment of severe depression, perform the act.

Picture the tree with its branches outstretched toward the sky, embracing the air with an almost ecstatic feeling of exuberance. Now visualize the weeping willow with its branches falling down, often near or into the water, and think of the person "bathed in a pool of tears." The drooping branches are comparable to the descending basic line in handwriting. We may say the writer's spirits sag, the heaviness which comes with depression causes the head to hang down and the arms, hanging heavily, remain inert. And in the handwriting too, the basic line descends, as in Specimen 46.

SPECIMEN 46

It is very unusual to find consistently rising lines in the handwriting of a person who feels he is not loved. It is love that produces hope and optimism. The person who feels totally unloved, unwanted and forsaken is most unhappy. In such a writer's handwriting we may observe signs of violence because of feelings of rejection. Certainly the t bar depicting frustration will be present. The handwriting may look dead, without color or variation.

9. Margins and Spacing

The margin seems to have had its beginning in those days when monks did manuscript writing. The thumb of the left hand was held in the left margin while the right hand did the writing and illustrating.

Today the margin has come to have a graphological significance. First, in looking at a specimen of handwriting we see it as a whole—the *gestalt*, the German term meaning the whole picture.

A page of writing with even margins on both the left and right sides, and uniform and even spacing between lines and words, is pleasing to the eye. It looks like a framed picture. The person who writes this way is greatly conditioned by the aesthetic demands made upon him by his nature—everything he does, wears and chooses in the way of possessions is dictated by good taste. From this we get the first rule for margins: a wide margin on the left reveals a strong aesthetic quality. We think of the writer as giving other people a margin. The expression "I gave him a wide margin" is rather common.

Voltaire's handwriting, Specimen 47, is a fine example of such an aesthetic hand.

Look now at Specimen 48. Where there is no margin at all, on the left or right, we may deduce that the writer crowds other people as he does himself, filling in every moment of his life as he fills the page on which he writes. He may fill it with people, activities or things. He might be a collector of old newspapers and magazines, a saver of pennies. (Some of these people are, in the words of the old saying, penny-wise and pound-foolish.) He is often compulsively economical when it comes to saving time, money and food. He may spend his energy lavishly, walking miles to save a few pennies on a purchase. He usually has something put away for the proverbial rainy day. And if he falls into a neurotic category, he will usually have a few dollars

A PAGE OF VOLTAIRE'S HANDWRITING
(He signs with an underscored V)

11.º fevrier 1765 · au chateau de ferney prar genêve.

My distempers and my bad eyes do not permit me
to answer with that celerity and exactness that my
duty and my heart require · your seem sollicitous
about that pretty thing call'd soul · j do protest
you j know nothing of it · nor wether it is, nor
what it is, nor what it shall be · young scolars, and
priests know all that perfectly · for my part j am
but a very ignorant fellow.
Let it be what it will, j assure you my soul has
a great regard for your own · when you will —
make a turn into our deserts, you shall find me
(if a live) ready to show you my respect and
obsequiousness.

V.

SPECIMEN 47

me the same type of analysis

~~to~~ you made for ▮▮▮▮▮▮▮▮

I find your work very fascinating

and hope that it can be of value

stashed away that no one knows about, even though he may be riding high on a financial wave. Many such people are obsessed by money because of a fear of the future, even though they may be more than comfortable financially. The lack of margins on both sides of the page will reflect this obsession.

So we have another rule: where there is no margin on either left or right we may say with reasonable certainty that the writer has a sense of economy in one or more areas.

Maid yesterday afternoon catching up h
loads of mail and other loose en
has been raining all day so it was
time to stay in. I brought dolls a
dress maker to make something for
the time in Washington — I'll need
my old things are worn and I'll
12 month — Also brought dolls, an

SPECIMEN 49

In Specimen 49 the margin grows wider as the lines fill the page. In a case like this we know that the aesthetic overrides the practical. The person starts with a desire to spend a given sum on something

70

but ends by spending more than he originally intended. Often such a person appears to be extravagant, and if the writing is very large, this is true.

In this specimen, there are signs of practicality although the writer's tastes and choices are aesthetically conditioned. The writer, a woman, is an artist, and the small writing with mental formations tells us she is keenly intellectual also. The vertical writing shows the prevalence of reason over emotion and the avoidance of sentimentality. It tells us of her selectiveness, and the widening margin also shows that she keeps a distance between herself and other people because of her aesthetic sense.

SPECIMEN 50

The writer of Specimen 50 starts with a margin but fills it in, showing that, in the final analysis, practicality overrides aesthetic sense. Confusion is shown in the way the y runs into the line below. It is the same confusion that causes the writer to remember later what should have been said in the first place. Good taste is negated as the available space is filled in.

It should be mentioned, too, that the person whose margin starts wide and narrows toward the bottom is someone who starts out lavishly and ends by becoming cautious. A good example is that of the woman who goes to purchase a chair. She wants one that looks beautiful, but she finally chooses something that will wear long and well, even though it is not as nice as the one she originally had in mind. She is like the marginless writer in that she cannot resist a bargain. Such cautious practicality will be reflected in a hand that also shows some cramping in the writing. We think of the writer as someone who gets the most for his money.

The spacing between letters and words gives us clues to whether the writer's viewpoint is narrow, broad, single-tracked, bigoted, self-centered, tolerant, expansive, pliable or generous. Where the spacing between words is inordinately wide, a symptom of paranoia or delusions of persecution is present. (It is as though the person stopped after writing each word and looked around suspiciously to see whether "they" were looking!) This is usually substantiated by other pathological signs dealt with further on.

Words tightly and angularly formed, as in some German script, reveal rigidity, efficiency, often scrupulousness, a sense of economy (corroborated by a lack of margin), and a certain lack of humor. Words made in garland-like formations are indicative of gentleness and gracefulness—the signs of the gracious person with a somewhat child-like and certainly an agreeable nature. (Not that all children are agreeable!)

Look at the spacing in Specimen 51. There is a contradiction here between the tight writing and wide spacing. This tells us the writer is rigid, repressed and somewhat paranoid, yet has a strong aesthetic quality. Such a person is restrained from acting openly and with real spontaneity. He is sensitive and overreacts many times, as the exaggerated spacing shows.

SPECIMEN 51

In Specimen 52 the words come close together without much spacing in between. This tells us the person is narrow-minded, thinks literally (signified also by connected letters in words) and is careful of detail (corroborated by the carefully dotted i's and crossed t's). This person hews to the line and lives in a tightly closed world.

almost impossible for me to chan
meet here. The arriving friends th
travel schedule all made out; a
not only be bitter to disappoint th
might take another nine years

SPECIMEN 52

The large writing of Specimen 53 shows extravagance at the very outset. The spacing between lines is disturbed by lower loops which run into the line below, telling us of confusion and self-centeredness. Dreams from a fantasy world spill over into the world of reality, and the writer must have things, possessions, concrete realization of those dreams. (The writer is a completely self-indulgent woman who is married to a multimillionaire. She is an exhibitionist who makes large gestures and finds concentration difficult.)

Here Ive go
again! Dont
pull the pun
ive me the

SPECIMEN 53

Any handwriting that is well spaced between words and lines shows organized thinking and is invariably indicative of executive ability, especially when the writing is large and the capitals are printed. This will be corroborated by signs of good judgment.

10. t Bars

Will and Intellect are one and the same thing.—SPINOZA

What are the elements which cause us to describe someone as a "strong character"? Or, the other way around, what elements, if lacking, lead us to call the character weak? Whether, as we observe human behavior, our viewpoint is philosophical, psychological or graphological, the answer would be the same—*will power*, that is, the extent to which the will is disciplined, and whether it takes a plus or minus direction.

Education of the will is something apart from the kind of education which means the accumulation of information. It has, rather, to do with intelligence. The intelligent person realizes that in order to enjoy living, his life must have some purpose. After he attains this awareness, will power steps in to direct his energy toward the desired goal. Foresight, self-discipline, judgment and optimism are necessary if he is to succeed.

The handwriting of the well-adjusted person reveals will power plus the combination of such traits as foresight, self-discipline and reliable judgment.

In handwriting, it is the horizontal strokes which indicate the balance in the character and determine how much will power and self-confidence the individual possesses. For this reason, the way the t's are crossed is extremely important. In addition, the horizontal final strokes on the ends of words give us a picture of the way a person uses his drive. (See Chapter 16.) If t bars have hooks on the end, the finals usually have them too.

There are least fifty different kinds of t bars so far discovered by graphological researchers. Human beings express strength and weakness in many ways.

Specimen 54, on page 76, shows the t bars that most often appear.

75

t BARS

Plus

1.
2.
3.
4.
5.
6.
7.
8.
9.
10.
11.

Minus

1.
2.
3.
4.
5.
6.
7.
8.
9.

SPECIMEN 54

Any other type you may see is probably a variation of one of these. Let us examine the t bars one at a time.

On the Plus Side

This firm, centered t bar shows balance, self-confidence, determination, self-discipline and attention to detail. It is the t bar we were taught to make in school.

Where the t bar flies away from the stem of the letter on the right, it shows animation, enthusiasm, often impatience to get things done. This might be interpreted as meaning that the writer rushes to finish a task which, in his mind, is already done.

This fly-away t bar also indicates a hasty temper.

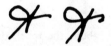

The looped t bar shows persistence. It also reveals a kind of perseverance which is instinctive rather than developed. Where the hook appears on the end, it merely augments the meaning, and we may say the person is very persistent. (Try imitating this sort of t and bar all in one stroke and you will realize that it takes persistence to do it.)

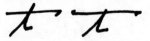

This long t bar with a hook on the beginning and end shows tenacity of purpose, the ability to hang on relentlessly to someone or something, often when the necessity for doing so is no longer apparent. (Here you can see that even the pen is loath to leave the paper.) This type of t bar is usually found in handwritings of people with a tremendous amount of nervous energy and an almost compulsive need to keep active.

This one, formed almost like a star, shows a kind of exacting persistence. It is also a sign of obstinacy, indicating that the writer forges ahead in what he wants to do, even in the face of strong opposition. This sign is often found in a handwriting where the same kind of angularity appears in the lower loop formation of the y or g.

In this t a combination of positive and negative forces is revealed. The t bar itself is strong, showing self-confidence, but the ending stroke comes down in a straight line—often below the basic line—and we describe the person as opinionated, willful.

This is the sign of the fighter, the rebel, the aggressive salesman, the domineering person who must have the last word in an argument which he often starts. We describe him as having a chip on his shoulder. Although we think of such aggressive characteristics as masculine, many women make this t bar too. It is often a clue to a defense mechanism a person has invented to cover up an inner softness, and it makes the writer appear to have the courage of his convictions. In truth, he can say "no" with finality.

Where the loop of the t bar appears *over* the stem, as here, it is also a sign of persistence, but it has the added connotation that the person writing it is *persistent about his personal wishes*. In such a person we encounter mild eccentricities of one form or another; the specific form they take can usually be determined by other signs in the writing.

The firm t bar that takes the shape of a bow and appears *in the center of the stem* shows excellent self-control. It is often associated with the sure, steady hand of the surgeon. Many athletes and people who construct things with their hands make this sign.

The t bar bowed *above* the stem might be called the sign of heaven. (It is the gesture of blessing a priest makes.) This bar shows the ability to curb primitive appetites and reveals a lofty imagination. A spiritual sign, it often points to the writer's strong religious leanings. Dedicated doctors and clergymen make it. If this sign appears even once in a hand which is otherwise negative, we may be hopeful that something good exists in the individual, and that he would like to be better than he is.

This t bar above the stem, straight instead of curved in the shape of a bow, reveals in the writer a spirit of adventure, vivid imagination, a tendency to reach out for the unattainable. We know that to him the grass seems much greener over the hill. The rich world of fantasy is often additionally indicated by high upper loops or high i dots.

On the Minus Side

The t bar that starts at the left but does not go through the stem of the letter tells us that the writer often starts things he does not finish. His will, somewhat impaired, does not have a positive voltage behind it. The reasons, more often than not, are of neurotic origin. We know that the writer is indecisive (although it may be only in one area); that he procrastinates; that he lives in the past some of the time; that he has periods of passivity. In some areas he is inhibited, somewhat repressed and lacking in self-confidence. Some people who make these incomplete t bars also make strong t bars. In such writers the will is often divided, a sure sign of the neurotic.

The bar close to the stem is a sign of repression which paralyzes the will so that the person seems to lack drive. He usually has strong guilt feelings.

The t bar that slants downward, but does not go through the stem, is also a neurotic sign, showing a combination of aggressiveness and weakness. The aggressiveness takes the form of arrogant weakness and we may describe the writer as petty, critical and fault-finding. He usually wants to give the impression that he is strong and purposive, but his strength ebbs before he has accomplished his purpose and he is often a person with terrific guilt feelings. The same incomplete downward stroke above the stem of the t tells us that the writer has forsaken reality for imagination, yet hovers at the edge of his fantasy world many times because he is not even happy there.

Except that this t bar does not slant downward, it has almost the same connotation as the preceding one. There is less arrogance, but the person is still unsure of himself and fearful of what his fantasy presents to him.

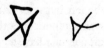

These t bars start out like the star-shaped t-bar on the plus side which reveals persistence. But since the first one does not follow over the stem completely, it is a sign of weakness. Although the writer has a capacity for persistent, capable and constructive behavior, something prevents him from exhibiting these positive traits. This is also a symptom of a paranoid or suspicious nature, but it must be taken in conjunction with other pathological signs.

The second t bar, through the stem, is similar in meaning. The writer takes the line of least resistance.

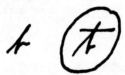

The first t here doesn't have a bar at all, but just a hook on the final stroke of the stem. It shows that the writer is sensitive and often lacks initiative in situations where he might encounter criticism. Where the person has succeeded in overcoming this kind of sensitivity, we have the combination of the hook and t bar (encircled) and we know he has overcome his weakness to some extent.

The stem with a loop, at the very outset, means hypersensitivity, and this is augmented by the t bar that does not go through the stem. This looped stem will usually be corroborated by a loop in the small d formation, as well as by other signs of sensitivity.

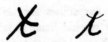

This t bar is the opposite of the bowed one. In a heavy hand it indicates earthiness and a measure of brutality. In a light-pressure hand—and often the t bar is lighter than the stem itself—it means that the person follows lines of least resistance. It is often accompanied by signs of laziness in slurred formations. By itself it means that the person drifts along instead of fighting obstacles; that he takes the easiest way out of any difficult situation, and in fact lacks a sense of responsibility.

Here the final stroke goes leftward on the stem of the t and tells us that the writer has no will of his own in some matters. He is being controlled by a will stronger than his own, which is his way of protecting himself. It is a form of withdrawal or introversion and his will is ineffectual when someone else, more controlling, takes over.

(It is safe to assume that in any handwriting where t bars on the minus side appear, the person lacks a sense of responsibility in some area.)

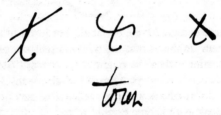

SPECIMEN 55

Specimen 55 shows still another group of t bars. The significance of each varies according to other signs in the writing.

Rising upward, this t bar shows aspiration, imagination, a drive toward a lofty goal. In a vertical hand showing snobbishness, this is the sign of the person with social aspirations.

This wavy t bar indicates good humor, love of fun and pleasantry, a jovial disposition and the ability to mimic.

The club-like t bar shows uncertain temper, cruelty and a capacity for viciousness which is not immediately apparent. When this sign is present in a muddy-pressure hand it shows that the writer is capable of physical violence.

A lance-like t bar shows sarcasm, terseness, a sharp tongue. It is usually corroborated by other lance-like formations, as in sharply ending finals in the single downstroke of the letters y and g. (This type of t bar is almost impossible to manufacture deliberately. Try it and you will realize how difficult it is to make this sign, unless you do it unconsciously while writing quickly and spontaneously.)

If in one specimen of handwriting you see a variety of t bars—some weak, some strong—it requires careful deduction to balance the plus against the minus. You will be dealing with a person possessing a number of wills coming into conflict with each other—a neurotic symptom.

11. i Dots

*It is notorious that the memory strengthens as you lay
burdens upon it, and becomes more trustworthy as you trust
it.*—THOMAS DE QUINCEY

Although i dots should be taken in conjunction with other signs in
handwriting, there are a few whose special significance will be explained on the following pages. Usually the meaning of the i dot will
be confirmed by the type of t bar with which it appears. The circle i dot
has a special meaning and may appear in *any* kind of hand, although it
most often is used by individuals who have artistic leanings if they are
not actually engaged in work of an artistic nature.

Since we are all taught to dot our i's, a good memory is revealed
when dots appear consistently.

SPECIMEN 56

The i dots in Specimen 56 are the different types that commonly
appear. Let us examine each.

i

The i dot that is directly above the letter, so that it is immediately obvious, tells us that the person has a retentive memory for detail. Most often we see this in the handwritings of detail workers, and it will usually be accompanied by a firmly crossed t bar which is evenly distributed on the stem. Such a person does everything he has been taught without much display of imagination or individuality. He is matter-of-fact.

ı

The i dot that is high above the letter indicates imagination. It is often found in handwritings where the t bar is high and often above the stem, which has the same meaning.

ı

Where the dot is really not a dot at all but resembles a tent, it indicates a critical faculty. This will be found in handwritings which are sharp and angular. The dots take on a form of angularity too. It is not unlikely that some form of the aggressive t bar will be present in the same writing, and there will certainly be signs of keen mental perception.

ı ı ı

A curve of one form or another instead of a dot is a sign of humor. These formations are sometimes whimsically referred to as "laughing mouths." They will be found in handwritings where there are other wavy strokes in finals or in curved t bars, corroborating the element of humor.

ı

The i dot that is somewhat on the right of the letter may be compared with the t bar that flies to the right of the stem. It means practically the same thing—enthusiasm and often optimism.

When the dot is on the left of the letter this usually indicates caution. It is often found in a handwriting where the t bar remains on the left side of the stem without going through the letter. This, however, is not *always* true of the t. Other corroborating signs of caution are discussed in Chapter 12.

Now we come to the circle i dot which shows there is something "different" in the writer, perhaps a mild eccentricity. Anyway, the *desire* to be different is indicated in this kind of dot, and the writer resorts to attention-getting devices of one form or another—either by a manner of dress or speech that is not strictly conventional, or by the kind of work he chooses.

However, it is also an artistic sign, often found in the handwritings of designers or people who work in the field of adaptive art. Usually these people are adept in the use of their hands—or feet, as in the case of dancers. It is more often than not apt to appear in vertical hand-writings.

If the circle i dot appears in writing that also has weak t bars, it is an indication that the writer is dissatisfied, and there will be other signs confirming frustration and unhappiness. It is safe to say that there is always a desire for some kind of artistic expression in the person who forms the circle i dot. He has an innate dislike for work of a routine nature, for the commonplace or ordinary, and is attracted to the bizarre, unconventional and unusual. Since the persistent t with the loop over the stem shows a mild eccentricity somewhere in the make-up, it may very well be accompanied by the circle i dot.

The unusually heavy i dot that is directly above the letter has an added connotation besides that of a retentive memory. It appears in a heavy-pressure hand and usually denotes aggressiveness which takes the form of cruelty. It goes hand-in-hand with the t bar which has the same meaning. In such a hand the final stroke on t's and other letters will also be blunt, showing an unyielding quality, bluntness and a lack of finesse. (This is discussed in Chapter 16.)

Here are the combinations of i dots and t bars that corroborate each other.

Specimen 58 is the handwriting of an interior decorator. The circle i dot shows her sense of design, while the small printed s tells of her artistic talent. The breaks between letters indicate intuition, and the long, swinging, rhythmic lower loops show a sense of the dramatic. All these signs show that the writer could readily design costumes for the theatre as well as stage sets. She became an interior decorator as a form of compromise, but if she had more initiative than the writing discloses, her drive and tenacity of purpose would help her to accomplish work for which her handwriting shows she is suited.

SPECIMEN 58

What about the person who does not dot his i's, yet claims he has a good memory? If he examined himself carefully, he would discover that he is really absent-minded about those details he considers unimportant. The absence of i dots where good memory is claimed will usually be corroborated by neurotic signs in the handwriting. We construe this as a person who has "blind spots." In other words, he closes his eyes to that which he does not wish to see in an unconscious attempt to shut out what is too painful to face squarely. To evade those incidents or experiences which he may be ashamed of, he pushes them into his unconscious. He may want to feel loving and tender toward someone (perhaps one of his parents), when actually there is an ambivalence of feeling—conflicting emotions, such as love and hate, admiration and hostility. He has been taught that he must love his parents. Therefore, to have hostile feelings toward them makes him feel guilty. He blinds himself to his real feelings and the result is—no dotting of i's! (Strange, isn't it, that the i's (eyes) in handwriting should have a relation to sight, although they relate to an inner vision more than the actual sense of seeing.) Invariably, the neurotic has such blind spots. The more insight he gains into himself (usually through psychoanalysis) the more he becomes aware of his absent-mindedness. This is a good example of how unconscious mechanisms are revealed in handwriting.

12. Small Letters (your a b c's)

How a person forms his small letters reveals how closely he has continued to follow the lessons he first learned, and shows the kind of intellect he has.

(There are some people who still write as they were taught, by the Palmer Method. But teaching techniques have changed and many schools today teach manuscript writing, which is really printing.)

The small letters a person forms show whether he has developed habits of obedience to prescribed routine. Many people feel safe when operating within a framework of obedience, for then they do not have to make important decisions, nor accept adult responsibilities. Those people who have a desire to express their individuality and a hunger for freedom break away from the letter forms they were taught and develop a style of their own.

The small letters reveal whether the writer is cautious, gullible, generous, talkative or reticent. Formations that were not taught in the classroom show signs of talent. We also begin to observe signs of the conditioning influences exerted in the home. Deviations from copybook form are especially noticeable in the handwriting of a talented child, often the "problem child" with a high I.Q. whose school marks may be below average. Such a child often rebels against the rules laid down by teacher or parents, possibly because there has been too much discipline exerted without the leavening force of love. (Any child will accept discipline when he feels he is loved!)

Let us examine the small letters and see what they tell us. *Tightly closed* letters mean caution. *Open formations*, usually at the top of letters, tell us there is an openness in the person which we may construe as generosity, and the open mouth means the person is talkative. In some small letters this same openness reveals gullibility, credulousness and vulnerability. This is especially true in the open-lipped small b, where there is a wide space between the loop and the final stroke.

If the writer continues to make the initial strokes he was first taught, it indicates a pattern of obedience in observing the details of what he does. Often where there are consistent initial strokes, the last letters on words will have an extra stroke too. We may say about the person who consistently makes both initial and ending strokes that trifles and details bother him, while often the more important problems do not affect him at all.

On the other hand, any elimination of a stroke, whether it is in the beginning, end, or the upper or lower loops, tells us that the writer is casting off unnecessary details and learning to come down to essentials. The simplified letter is a mental formation. Some people never eliminate the strokes they were taught to make. These are the people who continue to follow the rules they were taught to the letter. If they don't, they have guilt feelings, and this in itself indicates a lack of maturity in some areas. This does not mean that those of us who depart from the rules are devoid of guilt feelings, but our handwritings will reveal the methods we use to deal with them.

Various kinds of small letters are shown in Specimen 59. What do they mean?

Open-topped a's and o's, and s's open at the bottom, show a tendency to be talkative, and indicate generosity in the writer when his emotions become involved.

The same letters closed tightly with a loop reveal caution. When there is also a closed capital D, the writer is usually extremely reserved and often secretive.

The open b means credulousness. Closed tightly, it shows business ability plus caution. Without an upper loop it is considered a mental formation (together with the unlooped h and l). The last is an inverted b, which reveals inversion. It often appears with the inverted d.

The small c with an initial stroke shows attention to detail. An angular c means keenness and mental development. The round c indicates gentleness, as do other rounded forms.

Here we have a variety of d's. The inverted d shows inversion, often homosexual trends (sometimes unknown to the writer). The d with a loop shows sensitivity. With a space between the last two strokes it shows reticence. A long vertical stroke on the end of the d, which goes below the basic line, indicates obstinacy, a desire to control situations, and often a closed mind. The Greek d in the last two examples expresses culture in the individual and is often accompanied by the Greek e and literary g made like a number 8.

$$\mathcal{E} \, \mathcal{e} \, \mathcal{L}$$

The first e is the Greek e which means refinement when it appears in a handwriting without the other cultured formations. When the other signs of culture are present too, it usually indicates literary ability. The regular e which is rounded coincides with other signs of gentleness, and the e made like an i indicates keenness.

$$\curlyvee \, \mathcal{r} \, \mathcal{R}$$

The r, made quickly, by itself signifies little more than obedience to rules, but when it appears with the broad r in the same handwriting it indicates versatility. The broad r has the connotation of a strong visual quality in the writer. It is often found in the handwritings of painters, designers and even graphologists. It shows strong reactions through sight and often helps determine what line of work the person would be best suited for—depending upon other formations in the writing. A capital R in the middle of a word shows affectation.

$$\mathcal{s}$$

A printed small s reveals talent in the writer, as do other printed letter formations.

$$\rho \, \mathcal{r} \, \rho$$

The p which comes down in a straight line often shows good physical coordination; the p with the last stroke slurred points to some inertia in the writer; the p with a lower loop should be considered mainly for the loop formation and what it reveals.

$$\mathcal{m} \, \mathcal{u} \quad \mathcal{n} \, \mathcal{u} \quad \mathcal{v} \, \mathcal{r} \quad \mathcal{w} \, \mathcal{w} \quad \mathcal{x} \, \mathcal{x}$$

The small m, n, v, w and x should be observed for angularity or roundness; the y and z, just as the f, g, h, j, k, l, p (letters with either upper or lower loops or both) from the standpoint of what the loops reveal (discussed in Chapter 14). They will usually corroborate other findings in the same specimen of handwriting.

The *style* of the small letters—whether they are angular, rounded or both—tells us important things about the writer. If you study the letters m, n, v, w and x you will see whether a handwriting falls into the angular or rounded category. Many times it is both. Angular writing shows mental development of one sort or another. It indicates some keenness, certainly efficiency and often a rigid personality that lacks pliability. In many instances the very angular writer is an unyielding, humorless, exacting person.

The rounded garland-like look in handwriting tells us the person is pliable, gentle and often childlike. Take note of the roundness in the writing of a child. (If I were choosing a nurse for my child, I would be sure there were many rounded formations in her writing.)

Then there is the combination of roundness and angularity, where the bottoms of letters are rounded and the tops are sharp and angular. We deduce that the mind of such a person is keen, while his nature is gentle and tractable.

The following examples will illustrate the variations in style.

SPECIMEN 60

Specimen 60 is an example of the Palmer Method of writing—clear, legible, rounded. Although it was written by an adult, the roundness tells us the writer is childlike in many ways, obedient and tractable. The t bar in the word "handwriting" which does not go through the stem of the letter gives us a major clue to the fact that he lives in the

93

past, follows rules he was taught and is emotionally dependent. This can be construed as regression, since he was taught to make a t bar that goes through the stem.

If you will send me the explanatory texts for the numbers in which you are interested I shall translate them for you

SPECIMEN 61

Specimen 61 shows a combination of roundness and angularity (turn the writing upside down and you will see how rounded it is). We conclude that the writer's mind is developed since letters like m and n are angular, while the nature is still gentle and pliable.

Having been an amateur graphologist for a but never having had my own writing examin in knowing the opinion of a professional. Tho agree heartily with what you said. I feel, to

SPECIMEN 62

In Specimen 62 there is no roundness at all. The writer is rigid, exacting, methodical. The writing looks mechanical. He sees with the eyes of a builder as he structures his letters and words. Whatever softness may be in the nature is poured into a rigid mold and to the world he appears stiff and unyielding, as is the handwriting.

94

unusual degree. In fact in
all terribly concerned about
I hope that now that the
and presume, because of her,

There is rigidity of a different sort in Specimen 63, for something else has been added in the t bars above the stems. We are dealing with a domineering, demanding, cruel person who fantasies himself as a general. He must control every situation. It is contradictory to discover that the capital I in the third line is so very small in relation to the rest of the writing! We know from this that the writer's ego is really rather weak and that the fantasy is the determining factor. He dominates and overcompensates for his feelings of inadequacy in a neurotic, irrational manner. His approach is unrealistic, as compared with the preceding writer.

13. Capitals

The way a writer forms capital letters gives important clues to his taste, pride and feelings toward authority. They also tell whether he is vain, conceited, egotistical; modest, self-effacing, humble; old-fashioned, artistic, or just plain vulgar. They reveal whether he is conventional, rigid or pliable, frank or reserved, and whether his attitude toward other people is one of protectiveness or contempt.

The larger the capitals, the greater the pride. Small capitals reveal modesty, self-effacement, often humility.

The capital I tells something specific about the writer's opinion of himself as well as what he wants others to think of him. It reveals the kind of intellect he has, gives a clue to his talent, and together with his signature discloses whether he has an inferiority complex of one kind or another and has found compensation for it.

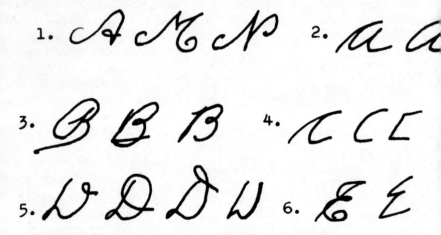

SPECIMEN 64

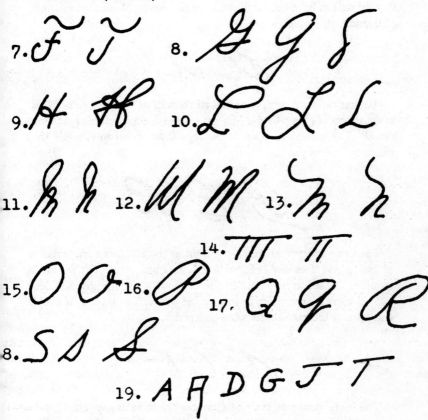

The capital letters in Specimen 64 appear most often. (The I's are dealt with separately.)

These are the old-fashioned capitals, the kind made during the hoop-skirt era. They reveal an old-world attitude in the writer; a respect for old traditions. They tell us the writer is conventional, protective and paternal (or maternal) toward the downtrodden, weak, childlike.

When these capitals appear in handwritings of young people they reveal
that the writers have been influenced by someone with ideas of a former
generation.

The first capital A with an initial stroke tells us the person uses this
stroke almost as a prop to give him pause in a situation before expressing
himself. The second A, open at the top, shows generosity, while the
roundness means pliability.

The extra inflated stroke on the right of the B shows some inflation
of the ego, as does any exaggeration in a capital letter. The second is
modified, closed at the bottom for caution, while the graceful look
tells us there is something artistic in the writer. The third B is simple
and open at the bottom, showing generosity.

The initial stroke on the first C means the same as any initial stroke
on a capital letter—a prop for the writer. The rounded C shows idealism
and gracefulness. The angular C tells us the person is somewhat rigid
and will corroborate other angular strokes in the handwriting.

The capital D open at the top shows frankness; another meaning is
that the writer finds it hard to keep confidences. It is a sign of oralness

like an open mouth. Conversely, the closed capital D shows reserve and the ability to keep secrets; the writer also keeps his own counsel, does not always reveal what he is thinking and dislikes probing on the part of others. The third D with a flying loop at the top shows capriciousness. In women it amounts to coquettishness; in men flirtatiousness. It is a sign of frivolity somewhere in the nature. The fourth D in this group tells us the person is somewhat phlegmatic. It is formed lazily and open at the top, indicating that the writer talks without thought of consequences.

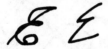

Here we again encounter the initial stroke on a rounded capital E, which has the same meaning as other initial strokes on capitals. Gentleness is also present. The angular E again means rigidity.

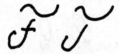

This type of capital F and T has a somewhat vulgar significance. The letters are ornate and tell us the writer likes "fancy" things which are not always in the best of taste. It is the conventional form we were taught to make in school.

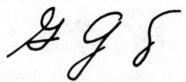

The first G is the conventional one which, in itself, has no special meaning and should be taken in conjunction with the rest of the writing. In the second one it is the size or form of the lower loop which is significant. The third is a variation of the literary g made like a number 8 and will usually be corroborated by the same type of small g in the body of a specimen.

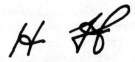

The simple H means simplicity of tastes and a firm ego; the involved letter tells us that the person gets himself into involved situations and is something of a strategist so that he eventually gets himself out of them. We find it also in the handwritings of people who are somewhat conniving.

The inflated top loop in the capital L expresses generosity; when it is inflated at the bottom it expresses vanity. Here the third L is simple, artistic and graceful and will be corroborated by other signs of artistic trends in the rest of the writing.

The incurve on the capital M and N tells us the writer has family pride and is sensitive. This is what any incurve in handwriting reveals.

Where the third mound of the M is higher than the other two, it tells us the person has a need to be in a position of authority in order to feel adequate. We find it often in handwritings which show other signs of neurosis, of inferiority feelings. When it is rounded at the top it means the person imposes his authority with a gentle technique; when it is angular, the person can assert himself in an exacting manner, making others feel his authority.

The graceful first stroke on the capital M and N tells us of good nature in the writer, of friendliness and a desire to be agreeable. More often than not, the strokes will be rounded.

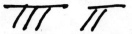

This is the "modern" version of the capital M and N, showing an aesthetic sense. It is often found in handwritings of individuals who are artistic, preferring simple rather than ornate things. The mind prefers essentials rather than clutter and unnecessary detail.

The simple, perfect capital O shows balance and clear thinking and will usually be corroborated by other such signs in the writing. The open capital O shows frankness, as in the open capital D.

The initial stroke of the P and inflation to the right mean inflation of the ego; the rounder it is, the more vulnerable the person.

The capital Q made like the perfectly rounded O has the same meaning of balance and clear thinking. The loop of the second Q is what is important. The capital R may be observed for graceful rhythm, an initial stroke and its size.

The printed capital S (as any printed capital) shows constructive ability; the second in this group indicates simplicity of a person who is mentally lazy; the third is the conventional Palmer Method formation taught in school.

$$A\ R\ D\ G\ J\ T$$

These printed capitals show constructive ability.

The Capital I

Apart from other capital letters, the I has a significance of its own. It is the keynote to the ego of the individual and often gives us clues to the personality which are not revealed in other letter forms.

$$I\ \ 7$$

$$I\ am$$

SPECIMEN 65

Specimen 65 shows some capital I's used by people of highly developed intellect.

$$I$$

This capital I made like the Roman numeral tells us the writer is constructive and capable of clear thinking. The severity of the capital indicates some severity in the writer—perhaps in his taste, if not in his thinking.

7

This capital I is really a single downstroke with a little cap on it. It reveals a person who can think concisely while keeping a slight lid on his thoughts, not saying all that he thinks.

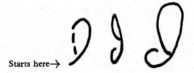

This single stroke tells us the person's mind can be clear and concise. The ego is strong and firm, and there is something masculine about the thought process in that it does not concern itself with detail but comes down to essentials. There will be other severe and simple formations in the same writing, and the writer prefers simple things as possessions rather than fancy trappings. It will often be found in a handwriting where the small h, l, and k have single strokes instead of loops, that is, in those letters we have come to recognize as mental formations.

Starts here→

SPECIMEN 66

The I's in Specimen 66 are different from the usual formation, because in each the first stroke starts from the inside instead of the outside. It goes around from left to right instead of from right to left. The way to be sure a person forms such a capital I is to watch him write. The meaning of such a formation is that the writer is a complete rebel. He is perverse, doing the opposite of what is expected of him. Such writers are the individuals who start out in life resenting parental authority and later often come to grips with the law. Writers of this kind of formation often possess some outstanding talent although it is impaired, many times, by a neurosis if not a psychosis. Some become emotional vagrants (alcoholics, for example), and a few spend a large

103

portion of their lives in mental institutions—unless their handwritings also show a capacity for self-discipline and some balance. In the latter case, the writer of such a twisted capital I might gain a reputation as an iconoclast or innovator, perhaps expressing what may amount to genius in one form or another. If you suspect that a writer is exceptionally unusual, ask him to write his capital I and see if he does it the inverted way. You may be discovering a genius, if all other signs in his handwriting corroborate this sign and also reveal a capacity for organized effort.

14. Loops

Ah, but a man's reach should exceed his grasp,
Or what's a heaven for?—ROBERT BROWNING

A loop is an avenue of emotion. More than that, it gives us a clue to the person's ideals and his world of fantasy. A wide upper loop reveals a person who expresses himself through his emotions in one way or another. Singers and musicians, professional or otherwise, make wide upper loops. In fact, all those who give obvious expression to their emotions do so. We might even go so far as to say that the person who is more emotional than intellectual makes these wide upper loops. That does not mean that all intensely emotional people make them. Much will depend upon corroborating signs. Emotional people are very sensitive, and in their handwritings you will probably see loops in the small letter d, and often the stem of the letter t will have a loop, too.

It is significant that when the heart is physically affected, as in heart disease, or a defective heartbeat, the upper loops show this in a ragged stroke at the top; sometimes the loop breaks and there is a space before coming down on the downward stroke. Many people do not know they have a heart condition if they have not had a thorough physical examination, so that seeing this sign consistently gives the graphologist a chance to sound a note of warning. If only one loop is ragged at the top, it may be the fault of the pen or a specimen written in haste. But if *all* are ragged, then look for other signs of illness.

If the upper loop is compressed instead of wide open, the logical conclusion is that the person is repressed, often tense, and does not open up or express his feelings readily. In his handwriting, you will find other signs of fear, caution and often tension.

Then there is the loop that is a mere single stroke—no loop at all.

This can be described as a mental formation. In the same handwriting you will discover other simplified letters. The writer has learned to eliminate unnecessary detail and can come down to essentials. Thus, in the unlooped small h, l, and b we have the sign that the person has a developed intellect. Sometimes you may find one or two such single strokes in a handwriting while loops are also present. This means that the writer is developing mentally, and may in time eliminate all upper loops.

You may also come across a loop that is squared at the top. Some of the other letters in the same handwriting may show this angular formation. It points to a measure of rigidity amounting to obstinacy.

The loop that looks as though its back were broken is a sign of unhealthy withdrawal and is often found in perverts and homosexuals who have not come to terms with their homosexuality.

The very high loop, often very wide and quite exaggerated, which looks out of proportion to the rest of the writing, tells us the person is visionary and lives a great deal in a world of fantasy. (This, too, will be corroborated by other signs.)

Remember that handwriting is an unconscious gesture which represents the strivings of the individual. Upward-reaching loops symbolize a dreamworld. The extent of the writer's reaching for the unattainable is determined by the height of the loops and other signs, such as the t bar which appears above the stem of the letter.

You will also come across the rather squat low loop which is not much higher than the small letters. Such a writer is in touch with reality, is close to earth and practical.

Lower loops, below the basic line, express the physical, sexual, materialistic, earthy demands made on the individual by his own nature. Long, rhythmic, wide lower loops indicate that the writer's physical urges are strong. This includes the sexual drive; the person is sensuous, emotional, has strong animal drives. There are, however, a number of meanings to this kind of loop, so let's take them one at a time.

First there is the loop you were taught to make. There is as much width, length and rhythm in the lower loop as in the upper one. The person writing loops this way has a fairly good chance of realizing his dreams because he does not overreach himself—his dreams are possible of realization.

Then there is the loop which is not a loop at all but a single down-stroke. The elimination of the final stroke indicates practical good judgment. A y that looks like a 7 and a g that looks like a 9 are often written by people who enjoy dealing with figures. They are practical and can deal with reality.

The lower loop that is squared is a sign of obstinacy, and often of mechanical ability, as though the writer were "squaring off." I have found this kind of loop many times in the handwritings of mechanical draftsmen who use a ruler in their work. Primarily, it means that the person does not give up easily when in pursuit of something he wants. (t bars will have the same square look in such a handwriting.)

There is also what might be termed a loop within a loop, as though the writer were doubly persistent. Here we have the compulsive person who persists even when there is no apparent need to do so.

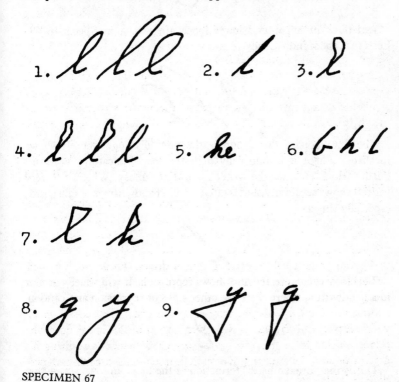

SPECIMEN 67

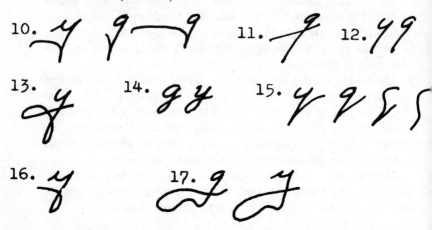

Variations in upper and lower loops are shown in Specimen 67. Let's take them individually.

The first loop in this group is the normally high one. It shows idealism. Where it is unusually high the loop indicates a visionary quality which enriches the writer's world of fantasy. Where it is very wide, it shows sensitivity, and is often seen in handwritings of musicians, especially singers.

This loop is compressed and shows repression. It will usually appear in a handwriting where there are other signs of repression and caution.

This is the "broken back" formation of the loop, and gives us a clue to something emotionally sick in the writer, as though his fantasy world were distorted.

The loop that is ragged at the top, lighter or broken at the sides tells us there is something wrong with the person's heart. When other ragged or broken formations show, it is time to sound a warning about the writer's health.

The small loop that does not reach very high into the upper zone tells us the person is practical, more down to earth than the fellow who reaches up in high loops. Other signs in the writing will substantiate this.

Here the upper loop has been eliminated so that there is just a single stroke. Such strokes in place of loops are what we refer to as mental formations. Wherever they are found, even if in the handwriting of a child or adolescent, we know the person has a capacity for uncluttered thinking.

The loop squared at the top has the same meaning as any angular formation—the person has a measure of aggressiveness, obstinacy and rigidity.

The first lower loop formation seems "normal," and indicates a normal interest in things in a world of reality. The second one here is exaggerated and shows a number of things: a sense of the dramatic; a greater than average desire for possessions; healthy physical appetites, including strong sex impulses. The primitive desires are strong here. Where the rhythm is quick and obvious, we have the sign of the athlete, the dancer, the person who enjoys physical activity.

The angular loop shows aggressiveness and obstinacy; when it is very wide this meaning is accentuated and a sense of drama is also revealed. The angular loop that is narrower will appear in a writing where other letters are compressed and show caution.

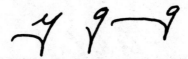

These are variations of the formation which expresses clannishness. (It is a backward stroke and connotes something that deals with closeness to family.) It also has the meaning of being exact, as has any angular stroke.

Here the person makes a single downstroke but adds an unnecessary stroke. Sometimes the writer learns to eliminate the extra stroke and exhibits his good judgment.

Good judgment is primarily shown in this single downstroke of the y and g. Mathematical ability is also present (the letters resemble the numbers 7 and 9 respectively).

This loop within a loop shows the kind of persistence which amounts to compulsiveness. The writer often continues doing something even after the necessity is no longer apparent.

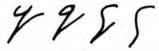

These short lower loops mean that the writer does not emphasize material things. When they are found in a light-pressure handwriting, or in one where the writing itself looks unsteady, we know the person lacks physical vitality and we look for signs of illness.

This is what we call graphologically the *altruistic* formation. The downstroke comes back to the right, as though the person dips down and then gives away something—of himself, of his possessions. It has various meanings depending upon other formations in the writing. It can give us a clue to masochism, a martyr complex or real and selfless generosity. But most of all it means that the writer has a need to contribute something. We usually find it in the handwritings of those who have made contributions in one form or another to the world; but we also see it in the writing of simple, complex and neurotic individuals, and we know that the writer derives happiness from giving in one form or another.

Here the writer starts to make the altruistic y but something in him— caution, fear, sensitivity—changes his course and he ends by closing the avenue within himself. The same handwriting will reveal caution and conflict to corroborate this sign.

111

These lower loops are broken. I have seen such loops in the hand-writings of people who limped. We may assume that any physical impairment of the lower limbs will show in some way in the lower loop formations.

Any other types of loops are probably merely variations of those described.

15. Zones

"*We are such stuff as dreams are made on.*—SHAKESPEARE

Man, considered a civilized animal, functions on an emotional plane from which he reaches out to his fellow man for love, understanding and approval.

In the *upper zone* of his handwriting, the kind of upper loops he makes reveals his dream life, ideals and fantasies. Other high strokes corroborate his reaching up. The *middle zone* gives us clues to how he copes with the reality of daily routine and the exigencies connected with practical life. We try to estimate how his actions affect other people. We can see, too, whether he is using his dreams as a blueprint for achieving the success he strives for, whether he has learned to function, without friction, in a world of reality. The work he does and the people he associates with may be part of a compromise solution that serves to fill his life in a useful way and helps him avoid both loneliness and censure of others.

If the physical demands made upon him by his own elemental nature are stronger than he can cope with in the normal course of daily living, he may be a person in conflict. This will become evident in the kind of lower loops he forms—they will either fill the lower zone or spill over into the space below it. He may be fighting "the world, the flesh, and the devil" and suffering from guilt feelings that come from the conflict between what his ideals (upper zone) demand that he do and what he actually does.

Or, he may effect a compromise between his ideals and primitive demands so he can function with some serenity on the realistic (middle zone) plane. If he achieves such a compromise, we refer to him as well-adjusted and we observe a similarity of size in the upper and lower loops, and uniformity in small letter forms.

However, few of us function in such a balanced way since we are not machines. The dynamics of the human psyche push us in various directions and cause us to be inconsistent. The result is that many of us strive to realize dreams which are often beyond our reach.

The *lower zone* gives us clues to how a person copes with his sexual drives and what effect his strivings have on both his fantasy life and the world of reality as he views it. Where there are extreme manifestations in any of the zones—if the middle zone is distinguished by an absence of upper and lower loops, or if the upper zone has extremely high or very wide inflated loops, or if the lower zone is filled with unusually wide and inflated loops which run into the line below—we may be certain there is a departure from the graphological norm. We then look for other signs in the handwriting to substantiate a suspicion that we are dealing with an unbalanced person.

Where emphasis is placed on the middle zone (as in Specimen 69) this gives us a valid clue to the realist. He may be a literal-minded, earth-bound, unduly practical person. We may assume that earlier experiences of a painful nature forced him to give up his dream life because of fears and guilt feelings. We will usually see signs of such inhibiting emotions in the handwriting.

The morbidly sensitive person to whom reality has become too painful may withdraw into his world of fantasy where he feels adequate. He may do this with the aid of an anesthetic (as in the case of the drug addict or alcoholic). Under the influence of the drug he becomes one with his dreams.

The realist, on the other hand, learns to accept his daily routine and to cope with it in a common-sense way, without allowing his fantasies to interfere. If he has imagination, he may use it to enhance reality, and we often see him writing a vertical hand with t bars above the stem of the letter.

In dealing with the lower zone in which the loops are so wide and long that they invade the line below, we may conclude that unrealized dreams of childhood forced the writer to seek a form of realization in a material world where emphasis is placed on possessions. These possessions may supply the power, comfort and sense of importance he did not feel as a child. Similarly, the overly high, inflated upper loop tells us of the fantasy-laden world the person often retires to, but how much influence it has on his world of reality can be deduced from signs of strength in horizontal strokes (mostly in t bars). These will reveal how much drive he uses to attain the visionary ideals which seem to dominate his life.

To get a balanced graphological picture we must observe the horizontal strokes as well as the vertical ones. This will reveal whether a person is dominated by his fantasies or is using his energy to realize his dreams. We must also determine whether his animal drives are so dominating that they throw him into conflict with the civilized demands imposed upon him by conditioning influences and society, or whether he has found it necessary to find substitutes in expressing his sexuality in a realistic world where so many sexual taboos exist.

The following examples illustrate the meanings of the zones in the handwriting of three individuals.

Upper
Middle
Lower

SPECIMEN 68

In Specimen 68 the *upper loop* reaches up into the space beyond the *upper zone* and tells us the person is visionary and has a rich world of fantasy. He is sensitive and emotional. The capital D is the same height as the loop and the first stroke on the capital M corroborates his visionary idealism. The *middle zone* shows fair uniformity of small letters, telling us of a capacity to deal with reality within the framework of his physically active behavior pattern. The *lower loops* dip below the area of the *lower zone* and reveal strong sex impulses qualified by the idealism, so that the writer seeks to project his ideals in a balanced form. We may say of him that he has a kind of balance and capacity for adjusting to reality.

Upper
Middle *au ly happy if I could give*
Lower

anything of that sort to you.
I have no doubt you could to me

The *upper loops* in Specimen 69 are unusually low. This tells us that the writer does not spend much time in dreaming and is not influenced by fantasies. Nor does he have any noticeably impelling sexual drive because of the absence of long lower loops in the *lower zone*. Emphasis in this example is on the *middle zone*, which tells us he is a realist—simple, unpretentious and modest. Signs of culture appear in the handwriting, as befits the professor of history he is, and he deals with facts with mental clarity, a measure of talent and a retentive memory.

h gan for your sending

Upper
Middle *along so promptly. I*
Lower

ourselves as others see
theuch. We have to study

SPECIMEN 70

In Specimen 70 we are confronted with the normally high upper loops which fit into the *upper zone*, telling us that the writer's ideals fit into a framework of conventional acceptance. But the exaggerated lower loops which spill over into the lines below tell another story!

We know that he dramatizes reality in order to compensate for having to cope with it daily; that he finds in things (possessions) what his desires in childhood did not supply; that he goes through periods of confusion when he is self-centered and subjective, although this is balanced by evident extroversion. His aggressiveness keeps him functioning in the outside world in areas where he encounters excitement; where the scenes may be changing to cater to his attraction to anything novel or unusual; where he feels impelled many times to become oppositional (as shown in the downslant of the t bar) in order to assert his physical prowess. And we see him in the role of the salesman or advertising man, with showmanship and ability to work in the field of publicity. In any of these fields, his exaggerated sense of values would give him a capacity to be useful in expressing his orality. If there were no signs of a conscious drive or will power, we would be forced to consider such exaggeration of the lower loop an indication of aberration connected with the sexual area of his life. What saves him is that the *middle zone* reveals small uniform letters and tells us that he can deal with reality, if necessary, although he colors it to be able to communicate with other people in a colorful, dramatic way. (He will stretch the truth to enhance a tale and could be a successful raconteur.)

16. Initials and Terminals

We all originally learned to make initial and ending strokes, but later they came to be used as props on which to lean while we decided what we were going to say or do next. In small letters these strokes indicate attention to detail. They are details which could be eliminated, and when they are, we know that the writer has learned to unclutter his mind of inconsequential detail. This is often evident in elimination of other strokes too.

The masculine component in handwriting often shows a disregard for what is considered nonsense by the elimination of extra initial and ending strokes. But the female of the species has formed a habit from dealing with all kinds of detail in her daily rounds as wife, mother, companion and housekeeper. Her writing will, more often than not, show a preoccupation with detail. (I speak of the woman in whom the feminine component is strong.) Consider the day of a woman in the home and observe what she has to do—her work is composed of all details. If she became as annoyed with details as a man so often does she would be unable to function efficiently in her home.

The *long initial stroke on a capital* (as in "Christmas" in Specimen 71) might represent a proud person leaning on his cane, so to speak, before making his entrance or speaking his piece. It is also an indication of less self-assurance than the person shows to the world.

SPECIMEN 71

Again, the *initial stroke on the beginning or the end of a word* shows a concern with details. Thus we find clerical workers making these initial strokes, but it is not only they who do so. People whose minds absorb the details of a situation and remember them often become more bothered by details than by important things. It is a fact, however, that as the intellect develops and gets down to essentials, it does not concern itself with what it considers unnecessary detail. Initial and ending strokes are eliminated, as are other strokes—the upper loops in the letters l, h, k, and the lower loops in the y and g. Most children learning to write make initial and final strokes, but if you see a growing child eliminating either or both of them, you may be sure the intelligence is above average.

Terminals

When there is a final stroke that is *flung downward with a whip-like ending* it shows a form of aggressiveness. The whip can be construed as meaning that the writer has an element of sadism and can be cruelly domineering. There will usually be other signs in the same handwriting to substantiate this contention.

Long horizontal strokes, often ending with a hook, show curiosity of a persistent kind (the hook shows persistence). This type of stroke means generosity too—a "giving out" by the writer. However, this same sign will also give a clue to a measure of possessiveness present. From this we may conclude that although the person gives, he also wants to receive something in return. It may be material things or it may be love.

Terminals which *rise upward gracefully* show a form of inspiration, a reaching upward, and are often found in handwritings of people with even or affable dispositions. They are never seen in angular handwritings, only in those with a great many rounded formations. The writers are definitely gregarious, need people, and get along well with them. They enjoy conversation and socializing.

Sweeping, graceful terminals which rise up and outward to the right tell us the person is generous, capable of making graceful gestures, and also has a sense of humor. They will often corroborate signs of musical tendencies—graceful rhythm, rhythmic lower loops and occasional formations that resemble a musical note or clef.

Short blunt terminals show abruptness, bluntness and often reticence. In a vertical hand, this may point to cruelty, curtness, rudeness or a tendency to be opinionated. If there is heavier pressure in the blunt terminals than in the rest of the words, we know we are dealing with a bitter, resentful and sadistic person. Where the final stroke on such a letter as the small d or t comes down below the basic line, we know the person is not only opinionated and obstinate, but capable of shutting a door, once and forever, on his emotions. It is a primitive stroke and shows a measure of unreasonableness, but we must look for other signs before arriving at that conclusion. Our suspicion will be confirmed if we find t bars which slant downward abruptly, telling us there is lots of "won't" power in the writer.

The ending stroke which sweeps to the left, when the entire writing is to the right, tells us that the person has a measure of introversion and returns to his past in moments of introspection. Such strokes give us a clue to introversion, even though all the other evidence supports the contention that the writer is an out-and-out extrovert! We may be sure that something in his past has an influence on him since he unconsciously returns to it in his thoughts, or he would not make this stroke in a leftward direction.

The following specimens show various kinds of terminals.

SPECIMEN 72

Observe, in Specimen 72, the whip-like finals in the words "analyze" and "yours." The sadism expressed by this kind of stroke is further substantiated by other black-looking downstrokes. We might refer to the writer as a "Simon Legree." The incurve of the small m in the word "my" indicates that he is personally very sensitive about others hurting him.

120

the other + young son are she working as secretary the

SPECIMEN 73

In Specimen 73 the long horizontal finals in the words "are," "she" and "the" (and the others flattened on the basic line) reveal the writer to be generous. This final also connotes curiosity. Notice the small printed s, indicating talent, in the word "secretary," while the broad r tells us the person is strongly visual. The t bars here are light in spite of dark finals, and the contradiction means that the writer has more ability than he gives himself credit for.

there has always filled

SPECIMEN 74

The final upcurves in Specimen 74 show the affable disposition of a gracious, gregarious person who dislikes living or working alone. The roundness of the writing further indicates an agreeable quality.

when you come

SPECIMEN 75

Specimen 75 has a variation on the upcurve. It is as though the writer were making a graceful gesture. It is also an artistic curve, and the writer would probably be good at making simple drawings.

enjoyed and benefited a

SPECIMEN 76

In Specimen 76, notice the blunt endings on the final strokes of the d's, as well as on the very end of the letter t. We may be sure the writer can be blunt. He is capable of cruelty and bad temper, which is held in check by a reserve indicated by the vertical angle.

a man beloved

SPECIMEN 77

The heavy, somewhat horizontal finals in Specimen 77 also show bad temper. We may describe the person as bitter and resentful, possessive and suspicious.

that is the truth

SPECIMEN 78

The final strokes in Specimen 78 take a leftward turn in three words. Although the right slant shows that the writer is outgoing, we can tell that he has a strong area of introversion. The formation in the word "the" could be said to resemble a protective barricade. Anyone who writes like this is, at best, a very sensitive person.

17. Connecting Strokes

> By reason, man penetrates to the farthest reaches of the scientific world; it is the microscope, field glass, telescope in which he sees the working of the visible universe. Intuition is the crystal ball in which man sees the working of the invisible universe. It reveals the face and spirit of things, while reason reveals their form and structure.—MERTON S. YEWDALE

Logic, which is reasoning that is orderly and consecutive, reveals itself in connected, consecutive letters in words, and often in connected words, where the ideas, like the thoughts, are tied together. Logic is concerned with evaluating evidence that cannot be readily disputed, and with drawing practical conclusions.

A logical person seeks concrete proof that can be demonstrated in one way or another, by facts, figures and often through the senses. How many times have you heard, "Seeing is believing"? Yet even our senses often deceive us and as in sleight of hand, the hand is often quicker than the eye.

Some people are so logical that they compulsively concern themselves with the *letter*, thereby missing the spirit or essence of things. We refer to them as literal-minded. Others who learn from experience may also be logical, but their minds have an added ingredient—intuition. These people see more in a situation or person than appears on the surface. In handwriting intuition is shown by breaks between letters in words. When we are confronted with a connected specimen which is written with light pen pressure showing sensitivity, and includes signs of imagination in either high t crossings or i dots, we can assume that the writer has intuition but doesn't trust it, and we say he must find reasons for everything.

Both men and women have intuition, although we have come to

accept the fact that men are mostly logical because most of our scientists are men. Yet we know that the greatest artists were men, too, and without intuition they could not have reached such heights of creativity. In them there was, however, a strong feminine component. In the general run, a man can function without intuition, while a woman without it is an anomaly, since she is closer to the primitive source of creativity and *needs* it. When we see the handwriting of a woman which does not reveal the signs of intuition, we are forced to assume that, somewhere along the line, she is emotionally blocked, and we will usually find signs that point to a neurosis.

When a break appears between letters, it has been made unconsciously by the writer. Since writing is an instinctive gesture, here the hand lifts itself unconsciously to allow a flash of intuition to enter. There usually appears in one handwriting signs of both intuition and logic, with some words entirely connected while others are broken up. This tells us that the person can deal with practical situations but also that he has some insight and understands more than the superficial aspects of a situation.

Where intuition appears in handwriting without the sign of good judgment, we know that the person's feelings take precedence over his reasoning. He forms impressions quickly. We must look for the reason why he does this. Often we conclude that the intuition takes the form of wishful thinking or suspicion, and we say the person reasons faultily because his emotions dominate.

If handwriting includes both the sign of intuition and exaggerated lower loops, it is probable that the intuition often leads the writer astray. He may judge from superficial evidence alone. For example, a person may see his neighbor driving a Cadillac and conclude that he is wealthy. In reality, the neighbor may be in debt up to his ears; he may have bought the car on time just to delude himself into thinking he was rich. If his handwriting were analyzed correctly, these facts would become evident. But first, the person making the incorrect judgment must see in his *own* handwriting the fact that the Cadillac releases in him the superficial approach he uses in judging. It is also possible that this same intuition which caused him to judge faultily may be a form of wishful thinking—the unconscious desire he has to own an expensive car himself.

When we see many breaks in a handwriting, it is safe to assume that unless signs of good judgment are evident, the person jumps to conclusions, sizing up people and situation quickly and sometimes faultily. When the writing is completely broken up in the connections, with printed (or written) letter forms, and it looks individualistic, we are dealing with an *inspirational* hand. Talented artists, musicians, poets, writers and thinkers show such consistent breaks. (See Specimen 81 on page 127.)

Often a person's work conditions his thinking and influences his handwriting. We find few if any signs of intuition in the handwritings of bookkeepers, statisticians and others who deal primarily with facts and figures. In a handwriting where the letters are connected but even one break appears, we say the person gets an occasional flash of intuition. However, chances are he doesn't trust it and tries to back it up with logic.

Where intuition does appear in the handwriting of a person who is engaged in dull, routine work, we assume that he does not approach even this mechanically. He may make an art of everything he does and perhaps have interesting hobbies through which he expresses his creativity outside of his circumscribed work life.

Intuitive people are more creative than those who are essentially logical. Even the scientist following the rigorous scientific method may occasionally make a discovery during periods of reflection when he receives a flash of intuition.

What do the following four specimens reveal?

SPECIMEN 79

Specimen 79 is the writing of the logical person. Connected words show consecutive or connected thinking. Small writing indicates powers of concentration, while the vertical, slightly left-slanted angle tells us the writer reflects before he acts. One flash of intuition is shown here in the word "living" between the n and the g. If he trusted it, he would not be wrong since the sign of good judgment is present in the downstroke on some of the ending y's.

friends love you looking forward coming to visit expect you to be m here in the Garde

SPECIMEN 80

The large writing of Specimen 80 shows a form of exhibitionism where the person likes others to notice him and his possessions. Imagination is shown in the t bar above the stem in the word "the," and intuition shows in breaks in such words as "forward," "visit," "expect," and "garden." There are no signs of good judgment, and since the exaggerated lower loops stress materialism we conclude that the intuition takes the form of suspicion. The writer's strong visual sense is shown in the broad r and in the oversized lower loops. The largeness of the writing further shows a lack of concentration and a tendency to make generalizations.

126

*You still have a very cultured
and dashing handwriting (mine
is indolent by comparison), but
you must beware of too much*

SPECIMEN 81

Specimen 81 is the *inspirational hand*. Breaks between letters are consistent. There are signs of culture, imagination and literary ability. Again, the small writing tells us the writer has powers of concentration. Such extreme intuition may safely be equated with clairvoyance. This man is a mystic, as sensitive as a highly strung violin that produces music only when touched by a master player. We might describe him as being "in tune with the Infinite," or the cosmic force. He is Merton S. Yewdale whose thoughts are expressed under the title of this chapter! He is an esoteric writer who is way ahead of his time.

*Your mail was
finally forwarded to me
several days ago — via West
Copake to the Penn. Stayed
over to have some dental*

SPECIMEN 82

There is a combination of both logic and intuition in Specimen 82. The handwriting is that of a physician, a good diagnostician, which he could not have become without intuition. Furthermore, this handwriting proves an old contention that medicine is as much (if not more) an art than a science, for essentially this might have been written by an artist. (He does paint too.) The capital S is printed, as is the small s in the word "some" in the last line, and the Greek d and e tell us he is a person of culture.

18. Legibility and Illegibility

No legacy is so rich as honesty.—SHAKESPEARE

In itself legibility gives us no real clue to the mentality of the writer. Many cultured and talented men and women, including some statesmen and musicians, write illegibly. The illiterate person may also write illegibly, but this kind of writing is easy to recognize because of its clumsiness and poor spelling.

Children make an effort to write legibly, since their entire attention is focused on the formation of letters. Among those who are disturbed, however, we often find lack of uniformity in letters and illegibility.

The detail worker attempts to write clearly since writing illegibly would mean he is not doing his job efficiently. He writes patiently and slowly. The slower the writing, the more legible it is apt to be. We find this kind of patience expressed in the handwriting of bookkeepers, elementary schoolteachers and even in that of some artists who do meticulous, though perhaps uninspired, work.

It does not follow that legible writing belongs only to people on a mediocre level of intelligence and creativity. The clear-thinking scientist, the laboratory technician, the mechanic who does skillful work (the watchmaker, for example), all write legibly. It is a sign that the writer is careful of detail. But it means more. Psychologically it means that the person wants to make himself clear in his communication with his fellow man, whether through the work he does, his conversation, or his approach to life. He prefers to hide nothing, and very often because of this preference he reveals his simplicity, often his naivete and gullibility.

Even though the converse is not necessarily true, illegible writing does belong first to the uneducated person. It may become more readable with practice or education, but education does not *always* improve its legibility.

A person may be able to express himself clearly, yet write illegibly. On the other hand his conversation might be awkward or he might appear inarticulate, due to self-consciousness or a speech impediment, yet he may still write legibly. Many times the person with a speech impediment is so aware of it that he overcompensates in his attempt to clarify his means of communication by writing a distinctly clear hand.

Where there is great emotional confusion, it is virtually impossible for the individual to write a clear hand. The handwriting itself appears disturbing to the eye. But this type of illegibility must be viewed in a different light, since it may belong to the borderline psychotic or perhaps the schizophrenic.

It is interesting to note that forgers write a characterless and extremely legible hand. The writing of the dishonest person will frequently have ordinary letter forms, yet appear illegible because of ungainly and often ornamented capital letters. Here we must look for signs of evasiveness, found in t bars which do not go through the stem of the letter, coupled with letters which are mere strokes. Another clue is in the small d made either with a loop or with a wide space between the two final strokes—the one that goes up and then down.

Dishonesty, per se, is difficult to discern from just a few signs in handwriting. But we may be sure that wherever there is a constant slurring of letters, many of which are not readable, the person is hiding something, and it may readily be some dishonest act. Honest people usually have nothing to hide, although our culture has forced us often to withhold information about our personal lives for fear of being criticized or misunderstood. It is a very serious matter when you are asked to judge from handwriting whether a person is honest. Even an expert may hesitate to say a person is dishonest, unless he is certain the handwriting definitely reveals that the writer cannot be trusted.

The high-strung, tense, nervous person often writes illegibly because of inner quaking which transfers itself to the hand. Restlessness may make it difficult for him to focus his attention on one thing at a time, for his nerves set up an irritation. To the discerning eye of the examiner, this person's writing will not be confused with that of the shrewd or dishonest one. There are, however, individuals who become tense because they are paranoid and suspicious. Their handwriting will also show evasiveness because of the fears which cause them to become suspicious.

Then there is the person who may write quite legibly one day, and the next be unable to read his own handwriting because of its illegibility. This is a person who may have extreme mood swings. When all goes well, he is relaxed and able to write calmly, yet when he is upset by some circumstance which stirs his emotions, writing becomes a difficult matter. The tension and emotionality which caused the depressive mood swing will show in both illegibility and rigid pen strokes. It is wiser for him to wait until the depressive mood has passed before writing a specimen for analysis. It is better still for the analyst to see two specimens, one written when calm, and the other when in a tense mood. This gives a more balanced picture of the individual, and often discloses reasons for the mood swings.

The following examples illustrate legibility and illegibility.

SPECIMEN 83

Legible writing (of any sort) tells us the person desires a clear communication with other people. Specimen 83 belongs to a person who can be definite and concise (angularity). The intuition (breaks between letters) gives a clue to the fact that the writer senses much that may not be obvious, and is often two jumps ahead of the other person. He may even anticipate what is going to be said. The strong desire here is to know the truth.

SPECIMEN 84

In Specimen 84 many letters are slurred. Where slurs appear instead of letters (in any handwriting) we have the indication of *evasiveness*. The person does not reveal himself although he may pretend to do so. You may think you understand this person, but something about him will always remain a mystery to you. He talks a great deal but in the end you discover that you really don't know him at all. His fantasy world is a rich one, as shown in the clear high upper loops, and he functions on the practical level with self-discipline. But he lives in a world of his own and few people can really evaluate him with the proper accuracy.

SPECIMEN 85

Specimen 85 is the illegible cryptic hand. As the eyes become accustomed to this writing, the letters become clearer. It is another way of saying that as your acquaintance with this person grows, you come to understand him better.

A handwriting where all the letters are uniform in size reveals a person who evaluates most things in a balanced manner. We say he has a fairly well-balanced viewpoint, although before we assert this, other factors in the handwriting must also be taken into consideration. Where the letters are clearly readable, we know the person makes no attempt to hide anything.

SPECIMEN 86

Where the letters grow larger toward the end of a word, as in Specimen 86, it is as though the writer blurts things out; we describe him as impetuous.

SPECIMEN 87

Where the letters taper toward the end, as in Specimen 87, we conclude that the opposite is true and the writer is diplomatic or tactful. (Often tact and diplomacy go hand-in-hand with evasiveness, although the motive is different.)

↓

Describe to me your latest and be sure no one will have

SPECIMEN 88

SPECIMEN 89

Secretiveness is indicated where letter forms are closed tightly. This is especially discernible in the capital D. Part of the word may appear within the capital letter, as in Specimens 88 and 89.

So wont you move to another apt in... and we will arrange a meeting as soon as I get out of here.

SPECIMEN 90

Dishonesty may be recognized by a break which appears in the

133

lower section of the a and o, and often in other letters. (See Specimen 90.) Such breaks may be visualized as money bags open at the bottom where the money falls out. These formations are made by people who write slowly and deliberately and possess mathematical ability. Such persons often gain employment in banks or work as custodians of money, where their weakness has an opportunity for full expression. Embezzlers have been known to make these formations.

19. Signatures

The way a person signs his name gives us a clue to the façade he presents to the world. Brilliant and truly great men often have plain signatures, although this does not always follow. People in the public eye usually sign their names with an underscore, giving emphasis to the personality. The great Sigmund Freud, whose handwriting appears later in this book, signed his last name with a small F.

When you have nothing more than a signature with which to work, you may, with diligent application, find in it many clues to the character of the writer, but it is better to have both the writing and signature for a complete analysis. There may be times, too, when a specimen is submitted for analysis without a signature. You may, if you are experienced, get clues to what the signature *might* look like from the rest of the handwriting, but you can't be sure unless you see it.

The signature may be different from the rest of the writing. It may look *involved* and indecipherable even though the writing in the body of a letter is legible. This is often because the writer tries to prevent his name from being forged or copied, although a skillful forger might be able to copy the most complicated signature.

When the signature differs from the body of the writing, we conclude that there is a difference between the writer's character and his personality. Perhaps the slant is different. In Specimen 91, the signature is vertical while the rest of the writing has a right slant. We conclude that the writer is more outgoing than he appears. He presents a reserved exterior to the outside world, and appears aloof, self-contained, perhaps even unapproachable. But if you became acquainted with him (depending upon how he reacts to you), you would become aware of the magnetism that attracted you to him in the first place (as shown by the

135

It was wonderful seeing you today and I hope we can meet again soon.

Dale Cromwell

SPECIMEN 91

underscored signature). If you got to know him better (if you are the kind of person with whom he could open up) you would discover that he is really warm and responsive; he built up the façade of reserve to give him time to choose, with discrimination, those people with whom he cares to associate and become more intimate.

Observe the body of the writing: the many breaks between the letters, indicating intuition, the talent shown by the printed small letters, and the "mental formations" all give us clues that the writer is extremely sensitive and keenly perceptive. It follows that so sensitive an individual must have felt the need to protect himself with a wall of reserve, for he may have feared being crushed by what Robert Burns referred to as "man's inhumanity to man."

Conversely, when the body of a specimen is written in a consistently vertical angle and the signature slants to the right, we must conclude that the writer has developed an outgoing personality—perhaps because of the demands of his work—while actually he is reserved and does not permit a ready intimacy on the part of other people.

In both instances, it is safe to conclude that the writers are endowed with versatility, and this will usually be substantiated by other signs in the writing and signature.

The *underscore* expresses self-assertiveness. It also gives us a clue to the type of personality the writer has—whether it is magnetic, forceful, whimsical, unique—or "odd."

Where a period appears after a signature, as sometimes happens, this is tantamount to the person's saying: "I have said it . . . it is final. Don't argue with me." Other signs in the body of the writer's handwriting will often reveal him to be exacting and critical of himself, but unable to take criticism gracefully from others. Invariably this sign tells us the person is supersensitive.

Let us observe a few examples of personalities familiar to most of us.

NOEL COWARD

SPECIMEN 92

Specimen 92—Noel Coward—is distinguished by its originality. It looks like a design. (Remember his play "Design for Living"?) We see in it an underscore that is a continuation of the last stroke. It is unlikely that we would hear his songs, see him act, or watch his plays without receiving a strong impression. His large capital N, certainly constructed with originality, shows that he is aware of his importance in the theatre.

KATHERINE CORNELL

SPECIMEN 93

Katherine Cornell (Specimen 93) writes a vertical hand, unusual for an actress. Actually, there is much of the introvert in her, and she often

137

views life realistically. Her acting is often intellectualized. She does not give out any great warmth though she is a hard worker, as shown by the long t bar, and her intuition gives us the clue to her artistry.

TALLULAH

SPECIMEN 94

Specimen 94 belongs to Tallulah Bankhead, who signs only her first name. She knows this will identify her since there is only one Tallulah on the theatrical scene. Notice her large capital T, the high upper loops, the break for intuition. We know from these that she is a talented person with a quick mind and a rich world of fantasy. The final stroke shows her curiosity, but because it slants downward it tells us that she has moods of depression which sometimes overtake her in spite of her acting cheerful.

HENRY FONDA

SPECIMEN 95

Henry Fonda (Specimen 95) has much of the introvert in him too. He is a person of culture, as revealed by the Greek d. Fundamentally simple, often realistic, he can be friendly while keeping a distance between himself and other people.

CORNELIA OTIS SKINNER

SPECIMEN 96

In Specimen 96, the heavy-pressure hand of Cornelia Otis Skinner shows positive force, sensuousness to forms, colors, music. She has an intensity held under control, as shown by the strong t bar. The underscore expresses individuality, and despite the reserve indicated by the vertical angle, we have here the sign of exhibitionism.

JAMES CAGNEY

SPECIMEN 97

The signature of James Cagney in Specimen 97 has not only the underscore but very wide lower loops. We deduce from these not only a strong sense of the dramatic, but a need to surround himself with *large things*. We might conclude that the exaggerated loop formation expresses his desire to find some compensation for the fact that he is small in stature. He makes large gestures to show that, in spite of his small size, he can be physically strong, potent, tough, aggressive. The rhythm in those lower loops tells us he is a graceful dancer and a good athlete, while the y at the end of his name that comes down in a single stroke indicates that his judgment can be practical and reliable.

JOSEPH McCARTHY

SPECIMEN 98

The signature of the late Joseph McCarthy (Specimen 98) reveals secretiveness. See how some of the letters are enclosed within his final stroke. The last, unique stroke goes *above* the stem of the letter t, and from this we conclude that he was a man of vivid imagination whose fantasy world sometimes dominated his thinking. Whether it was a positive or negative world, we are unable to tell from the signature alone. We know he could be blunt and outspoken, and this is confirmed by the e in the first name which is larger than the other small letters. His caution—shown in the closed a and o—could be construed as a distinct contradiction to his bluntness. We may say, therefore, that here was a man who was cautious and secretive, yet wanted to give the impression that he was direct and fearlessly outspoken. The large capital J is a clue to his personal vanity, and the small r in his last name, almost imperceptible, indicates that he was not always clear in his communication with others and corroborates the signs of secretiveness and caution.

DAVY CROCKETT

SPECIMEN 99

Specimen 99 is the signature of Davy Crockett, who was so popular with the younger generation recently. His signature tells us that he was quite an exhibitionist, greatly concerned with appearances. (Remember the fur-tailed hat?) The open capital D reveals that he was a frank, outspoken person, and the long t bar shows that he had determination and will power. An adventurous person with many of the elements of the showman, his personality was as unique as the underscore in his signature. This personality had its influence for a period of time—as is generally true of most people who make the underscore. Such individuals will usually stand out in a crowd. If you hear a loud voice and see someone making gestures to attract attention to himself, don't be surprised if he underscores his signature!

JUAN PONCE de LEÓN

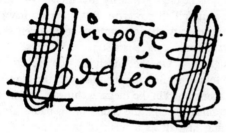

SPECIMEN 100

Legend has it that Ponce de León discovered the "Fountain of Youth." His unique signature (Specimen 100), which looks like a design, gives us clues to his bizarre and interesting personality. We might describe this signature as having boundaries within which the writer functioned. We might even construe the markings on both the left and right sides as foliage separating the island on which he lived from the rest of the world. (They also look like embellished dollar signs.) We see an elaborate underscore which tells us he was aware of his power and wanted others to recognize it too. Would he have been recorded in history if he hadn't been unusual? There is power, energy, fight, determination indicated all through the pen strokes. This signature was, no doubt, written at the height of his power.

SPECIMEN 101

If we were to compare the signature of Gamal Abdel Nasser (Specimen 101) to a map, we might say he was, more or less, an island unto himself. His name appears as though within a frame. (The fact that it was written from right to left doesn't matter.) It is an individualistic framework such as belongs primarily to a dictator—a man who would like to consider himself all-powerful. But there are flaws in his armor, for while he has tenacity that amounts to aggressiveness (see the hook on the downward stroke), there is also passivity caused by fear. Fear of failure, we might say. On the one hand, we are confronted with a deliberateness found in the typical sadist, yet the contradiction arises in his masochism wherein he negates himself. This shows in the horizontal line going through the center of his name, almost as though he were stabbing himself as a form of punishment for his brutality toward others.

The power drive within him is, therefore, diluted. But to the world he is purposive, ambitious, sometimes unapproachable, yet he has the charm of the vertical writer! The wide upper loop-like formation reveals his orality, the horizontal stroke at the right shows a strong acquisitiveness plus possessiveness, and the extremely heavy pen pressure tells us of a sensuousness to forms, colors, music. If we were to draw a pictorial inference from the pen marks, the feeling is that of an architectural structure, original in design, but not clearly understood by any but a choice few. He is something of a pretender, mainly because it is important for him to hide his real feelings. He can be either a cold, hard, unrelenting opponent, an obstructionist, or a little boy acting out his childhood fantasies in a drive to win in his pursuits singlehanded. He is a man to be reckoned with—one not easy for the observer to fathom.

142

20. How to Estimate Compatibility

I love him because he loves the things I love.—EMERSON

If you are a woman about to marry, how are you going to know for certain that the man you have accepted because he is generous, attentive, protective, ambitious to succeed in his work, is *really* all those things he wants you to think he is? Perhaps you suspect that he sometimes puts on an act, or is not totally honest. You may say, "My intuition tells me something." Do your doubts arise from self-doubt or from his occasional little gestures which you suspect are not sincere?

You want to build a harmonious, lasting relationship. Does his handwriting reveal him to be capable of sustaining any relationship? Do you have traits in common, do you complement each other, or are you acting out a childhood behavior pattern in your choice of this particular man? Is he looking for a mother, or is he mature enough to assume responsibilities? Are you both capable of a give-and-take relationship, or will one of you give while the other takes?

If you are a man, you must also evaluate your fiancée's qualifications for making you happy. Many engaged couples have found the answers to their questions through handwriting analysis. Examining both handwritings may answer some of your questions and give you clues to what you might expect. What *should* each of you expect from the other for mutual happiness? What makes for compatibility in any human relationship, whether it be a friendship between two men, two women, a business partnership, a give-and-take between neighbors?

In marriage, the element of sharing is important. Beginning on the level of sexuality, it should permeate every area of day-to-day living. There should be a capacity for two people to talk things out frankly, again beginning with the sexual area. While there must be common interests, there may also be areas in which only one has interests, and each partner should be free—even encouraged—to pursue them.

143

The financial aspect of marriage must be considered too. At the outset, the handwriting of one of the partners will reveal a better money sense, and it should be agreed who will handle the finances. This may save arguments in the future, and many marriages stand or fall on money matters.

The following groups of specimens were written by people who were considering marriage.

SPECIMEN 102

SPECIMEN 103

Specimens 102 and 103 tell us at a glance that both writers lean in the same direction. They have a common interest in other people, and possess similar views—both are even somewhat puritanical, in a sense. Both writings tend toward narrowness of a conventional sort. This couple could see eye to eye in an intimate relationship. A mutual understanding could develop without much effort, and they would live in their circumscribed world, each taking his (or her) duties seriously. There might not be a great deal of excitement in their lives, but by the same token neither would there be much friction. Specimen 102, the woman, has a heavier pen pressure, telling us she has more physical vitality, yet there are signs of passivity in the t bar which ends in a hook on the upstroke. The man's writing shows persistence in some of the t bars and spirituality in others, so that he would make an effort to control unruly impulses. I consider these two people compatible enough to make a success of their marriage.

enough away from Hugh t serve as the prescribed separation? He would keep

SPECIMEN 104

isible thing for me to do — but this it a normal occasion, is it? and would feel too unnatural if I did other. After all, Time is a very relative

SPECIMEN 105

In Specimens 104 and 105 there is an appreciable difference in temperament and intellectual approach, yet there is still a capacity to develop a common bond. The angle in both is one of reserve. They both have imagination—hers (Specimen 104) is shown in very high loops; his in the t bar above the stem. He is a thinker, indicated by the small writing with its intuition and imagination; she is passive and when she acts it is in a mild and unrushed way. Her pen pressure is

145

light, showing her sensitivity, while his is darker, telling us he is more intense although he is also reflective and controlled. She would respect his intellectual prowess, while he would find in her gentleness something to admire. There is enough difference between them to make their relationship stimulating and interesting without causing tension or friction. He is more mature than she is and would assume responsibilities, while she would smooth out wrinkles in any complicated situation that arose because she could be calm, patient and gentle. Both have a sense of humor, important to the success of any marriage.

Seriously though — I would very much like to have the study made and would love hearing from you soon again. Wish that you were here to enjoy this perfect

SPECIMEN 106

writing analyst you were referring to at you broadcast. It is conce

SPECIMEN 107

The writers of Specimens 106 and 107 would definitely be incompatible in temperament, their approach to life and their viewpoints.

He (Specimen 106), is withdrawn, as shown in the left slant. He is intuitive and artistic, yet undemonstrative. She, on the other hand, is impulsive and demonstrative. She needs people and seeks their companionship, while he often prefers to be by himself. Hers is a foreign hand (this is obvious to the expert examiner), although the g made like number 8 tells us she can adapt herself to new places. He, as a person of unusual tastes, must have been attracted to her because of her foreign accent (perhaps) and exuberance. Yet in the close proximity of marriage, she might readily get on his nerves. It would not be advisable for these two people to enter such an intimate relationship, although they could enjoy each other's company occasionally. They are much too different and the gap could not easily be bridged.

SPECIMEN 108

SPECIMEN 109

The writers of Specimens 108 and 109 are opposites. His tiny, microscopic writing (Specimen 108) belongs primarily to the hermit who often prefers to live alone. Her large writing tells us she is extroverted and needs people most of the time in order to function happily. Imagine two such people married! It would be tragic, for he might readily withdraw into his shell to think, while she, with a need for conversation, affection and action, would feel left out and starved for companionship. He is apt to observe her as a scientist observes a bug under a microscope, and she could never really *reach* him.

It does not take much experience as a graphologist to see that these two people are much too different to reach a mutual understanding and have a happy union. Marriage is not important to him; it is to her. He could be happy living with his thoughts, his books, his preoccupation with theory; she, conversely, needs someone who is more extroverted— a person whose handwriting has a right slant, more signs of sociability and less of intellectuality.

21. The Evolution of a Personality

> My heart leaps up when I behold
>   A rainbow in the sky:
> So was it when my life began;
> So is it now I am a man;
> So be it when I shall grow old,
>   Or let me die !
>
> —WILLIAM WORDSWORTH

As people grow and develop, their handwritings change too, reflecting the personality changes that take place. In this chapter we shall observe the handwriting of one individual written at different times in her life, examining the changes and developments, the effects of experience and environment.

The writer was 11 years old when Specimen 110 was written. She was the youngest child of a large family and her parents expected her to outshine her many brothers and sisters, to be more perfect and productive than all of them. And she was bright. At 9 months she walked and talked. At 11 years of age she finished elementary school. This specimen was written when she was entering high school.

at his plantation
to the privation he
and his soldiers
at Valley Forge duri

SPECIMEN 110   Age 11

149

She had been a bright obedient pupil in elementary school. She skipped grades, won a certificate for excellence in writing the Palmer Method and later won a gold medal in an art contest. She felt she had to excel in everything she undertook; *she had to be at the top.*

Let us look at her handwriting. First we notice the clear, well-spaced arrangement of her words; the careful crossing of the t's and the meticulous i dots. She obeyed the rules, remembering them to the letter. Her memory became one of her outstanding assets.

Her t bars are *above* the stem of the letter, giving us a clue to a vivid imagination, a rich world of fantasy into which she retreated many times, because as the youngest of a large family she felt she did not get the love and attention her nature needed and craved. She had to share with many others what her mother had to give. Her mother was undemonstrative and appeared "cold" to this child.

In her world of fantasy, she was loved, wanted, free to imagine herself an only child with all the attention given such a child. The broad r in such words as "privation" and "Forge" gives us another important clue. She was strongly visual and what she *saw* at 11, and probably earlier, too, was etched on her impressionable mind for the greater part of her life. The medium-heavy pressure shows a sensuousness to forms, colors and music which gave her memory an added dimension. She remembered music and played by ear; she loved colors. She read a great deal and identified with the happy characters in the books. She was an optimistic child, as shown in the tendency for the basic line to rise. But her home life was not a happy one and she felt isolated and rejected much of the time.

She left home at about the age of 17. She went to college, but did not continue because she began to rebel at routine and textbooks. Her mind sought an avenue through which she could express her individuality.

So, at the age of 19, we see in her handwriting (Specimen 111) the sign of the rebel—a downward stroke to cross the t's. The high t crossings she used to make, indicating her world of fantasy and corroborated by high upper loops, were replaced by high i dots, also showing imagination. But there is a new development in her at this age. It is cultural. She broke away from the Palmer Method d and e she had learned, and formed the Greek e; the d was beginning to take on the Greek formation, as in the words "today" and "tired." Further, a new formation appears—the one we have come to recognize as the sign

SPECIMEN 111   Age 19

of altruism—in the last upward stroke on the letter y in "today." We
have said it is a clue to the person's need to *give*, and indicates an
interest in the welfare of other people, especially when it appears in a
handwriting that slants to the right. Her fairly light pen pressure
coupled with the uncrossed t in the word "get" tells us she was very
sensitive. The roundness of the entire writing reveals her gentleness,
pliability and receptivity to experiences. She was a girl who needed
love and gave it. Many times she gave in an unconscious desire to "buy"
love, because as a little girl she felt she had not received enough. She
was so eager to be liked and approved of that she often gave injudiciously.
(There is no evidence of good judgment in the writing.)

In this small bit of writing, the spacing is quite uniform and the
speed obviously rapid. The evidence is that of a person learning to
think quickly and in an orderly manner. But she was still credulous,
trusting, sentimental, and therefore dominated much more by feelings
than by intellect.

In the three intervening years, she had a variety of experiences. She
worked in an office, taught foreigners English, wrote lyric poetry and
worked on a newspaper. She contracted her first marriage which
foundered on unsure ground, and then decided to study art. Specimen
112 was written while she was an art student. The change is obvious.
First, we see the angle has become vertical. This tells us that since she
found no fulfilling outlet in emotional attachments, she sought to

151

*In memory of the ma
pleasant and educationa
hours I spent with yo*

SPECIMEN 112   Age 22

express herself in some form of art. As an idealist with a rich fantasy world, she was unable to cope with reality. Here the t bars soar above the stem of the letter; the small s is printed. The capital I is different from the one she was taught to make in school, telling us she sought a means through which she could express her individuality. The little ending uncrossed t that comes up in a hook is a clue to her sensitivity, but it also tells us of a lack of initiative, a form of feminine passivity. Words are broken up and the spaces tell us that intuition had developed and she no longer followed the letter of rules taught her. Her mind became keener, as shown in the sharp, angular tops of letters. But turn the writing upside down and you will see how rounded the bottoms are.

While her mind became sharpened by a greater awareness, her nature was still pliable and responsive, though more reserved in its expression. The basic line still runs uphill, revealing her optimistic view of life despite her disappointments.

The altruistic "y" is more evident here. It is as though she were saying, "I will make my contribution in the form of art." She felt, because of her unhappy marriage, that she had failed as a woman. Although one of her drawings went on exhibition in the art school where she studied, she still yearned for love, and at the age of 24 her writing once more took on a rightward slant. Art did not fill the need for human love, and by this time she had divorced her husband.

With the divorce from a man who disillusioned her because he could not live up to the very high ideals she had set, her handwriting revealed major weaknesses two years later. In Specimen 113 it seems as though all the props had been taken out from under her. The conspicuous

152

*don't know what it's
about. But it looks
a long season. The t
idle one for this le.
bambino however. A*

SPECIMEN 113   Age 24

lack of t bars shows that she had lost her initiative and was drifting. All her o's are closed—she had become overly cautious because of her experiences. Even the small b's in "about" and "bambino" tend to be closed at the lip—almost as though something closed in her and her lips were sealed! Her talent still shows in the repetition of the small printed s. The capital B in "But" has a pleasing line which looks almost like a floral design. No altruistic lower loop here; instead, we see the beginning of a compulsion where the g is made with the return stroke in "long," and the lower loop in "for" just about clears the line below, but not entirely. The capital T has a rhythmic quality and gracefully covers the stem of the letter in "The." We see here a desire to get away from the Palmer way of writing the capital. The pen pressure is light and we construe this to mean she had developed an even greater sensitivity, especially because of the "touchy" t that has nothing but an upstroke with a small hook on it.

Examine the words apart from the basic line. Notice how "it," "long" and "bambino" tend to slant downward, revealing moodiness and unhappiness, even though the basic line itself slants upward. We see she still was hopeful and optimistic in spite of her tendency toward despondency.

Now look what happened here! Specimen 114, a fragment from a diary she kept, was obviously written *in desperation*. She was most unhappy, full of turmoil and conflict, and there is a kind of fury in the

SPECIMEN 114   Age 26

final stroke of the word "crazy." As a little girl and a growing woman
she was usually meticulous about keeping her mental house in order
(as shown in the careful spacing in earlier specimens) but now there is
an emotional crisis. She had strength, as seen in some rather strong t
bars, and was putting up a fight. The signs of talent are not to be
overlooked, except that here she dramatized herself! This shows in
the long lower loops, some of them running into the line below, which
also has the connotation of self-centeredness, a "stewing in her own
juice," as it were.

Disturbed though she was, something constructive was being born,
for some of her t bars show a tendency to bow. We will see in the later
specimens what this "spiritual" sign resulted in. Had it not been for
this sign, she might have readily destroyed herself. The emotional
storm was raging, but here a kind of energy shows in the speed of the
writing. A measure of determination is present too, despite the obvious
hysteria, even though the wide spaces between the words give us a
clue to paranoid trends.

SPECIMEN 115   Age 28

154

Doesn't this handwriting (Specimen 115) look like the calm after a storm? It took the subject four years to arrive at a more philosophical attitude toward life than she had during her emotional crisis. Suffice it to say that this sample obviously shows strong spiritual overtones, almost as though she were going through a transcendental period.

True, she had withdrawn into herself as shown by the small writing; emphasis is also on intellectual development. Cultured formations of the Greek d and e, a variation of the literary g, signs of intuition in breaks between letters, and the high t crossings, all tell us she was concentrating on a literary trend. (At this time, she wrote her first book.) The unlooped b and h are further evidences of mental development, and the altruistic formation of the y in "really" has returned once more to tell us that she was again interested in making her contribution through her natural talent. This time instead of in an art form, it was in a literary one. But she became more introverted. In effect, she might be saying, "I loved and lost so I will write about it and think about it, but no one will be allowed to come close to me for this could only mean I will again be hurt and rejected."

Five years later we see her more humanized. The emotions are again in evidence in the heavier pen pressure of Specimen 116. There is also,

SPECIMEN 116   Age 33

however, a form of rigidity expressed in the evident self-control revealed by strong, bowed t bars. This is the sign which gave her strength to carry on when her ship was foundering. She hung on (see the hooked t bar indicating tenacity).

155

By the time this specimen was written, she had one book published and was working on another. She had had a modicum of success and developed more poise and self-confidence in relation to her work. She learned to come down to essentials instead of wasting time on unnecessary detail (there are no initial strokes). Further, there is no trimming on the capital I. This severe formation in this kind of a hand tells us she became severe with herself. (The masochism expressed in this handwriting began to show when she first penned her altruistic formation at the age of 19.)

Some i dots have the shape of a tent, telling us she became more critical in her observations of others and of herself. Again we see the return of uniform spacing and generous margins. We are now confronted with a woman of culture and emotional intensity, sensuous to forms, colors and music. We must suppose that she superimposed self-control in order to accomplish anything creatively. Her real emotional problems remained unsolved; they were merely pushed back into her unconscious to rear their heads in another emotional alliance.

She married again—but this is another story. We can only assume from the signs of masochism in her handwriting that she must surely have been attracted to the kind of person who would reactivate this neurotic element in her. She would be doomed to *give* because of a need to be loved, but whether she received as much in return could only be revealed by an observation of the handwriting of the man she married.

Today she is functioning constructively in relation to the outside world. She has come a long way from the little girl of 11 who first obeyed, then rebelled at parental authority; rejected her family because she felt rejected; suffered disillusionment through all her emotional experiences; and finally found some relief for her yearning when her talent led her to be accepted by the world. All through these seven specimens the common denominator is imagination, sensitivity, a retentive memory, curiosity and a need to express herself as an individual. Whatever crises she may go through in the future, we may be certain (since we see the g made like an 8 and the hooks on t bars) that she will adapt herself to changing circumstances, hang on to life, and ultimately land on her feet like the proverbial cat.

It is not only the passage of time that can bring about changes in personality and character. A drastic change in a person's physical condition or a severe traumatic experience can effect a dramatic personality change that will, of course, be reflected in the handwriting.

Specimen 117 is the handwriting of Admiral Horatio Nelson before and after he lost his right arm.

HORATIO NELSON

Written with the right hand

Written with the left hand

The rightward-flowing specimen, written spontaneously, reveals the outgoing, extroverted, sentimental nature of a man of action. Although signs of intuition appear in breaks between letters, the tying of two words together and the unbroken words tell us he could think logically, that his ideas followed one another consecutively. The capital H in his signature belongs to the strategist—the person who gets himself into involved situations but, through some form of strategy, can emerge.

The bowed t bars reveal his self-discipline. The g made like an 8 is a sign of his interest in literature and his capacity to express himself in writing. In spite of the courage, strength and self-control indicated, his heel of Achilles was his sensitivity in the emotional area—and a clue to this appears in the hooked stem of the last t in the word "that," instead of a t bar. The continued stroke on his name, forming an underscore, tells us not only of his persistence but reveals a positive personality. The high upper loops tell of his idealism and give us a glimpse into a man who had a rich world of fantasy which often set off the spark of his sentimentality.

After Nelson lost his right arm in battle, his writing took on a vertical angle. He became more realistic and reflective. He held a rein on his sentimentality. His intuition developed further through reflection, as shown in many more breaks in words, especially "success." We see something else here—one s is printed while the others fall into a conventional pattern. Two different s's in a word are (remember this) a sign of versatility. His capital letters became simplified. No longer having any use for strategy, his life became simpler, too. In this piece of writing, the bowed t bars tell us he retained his self-discipline. Examine the word "battle," written with both the left and right hand, and see how the formation of the double t is exactly the same in both specimens despite the difference in angle. Further, the Greek d and e, coupled with the g made like number 8, are a combination which always reveals— in no matter what kind of a hand—literary ability. His talents took an intellectual turn as he was forced in upon himself through his physical impairment. He became more the realist, less the sentimentalist, and the old-fashioned capital N in the signature gives us a clue to a return to some old-fashioned, conventional concepts.

22. Signs of Illness -- Emotional and Physical

Conscience does make cowards of us all.—SHAKESPEARE

Before attempting to analyze the handwritings of emotionally disturbed or physically sick people, you must become proficient in evaluating the signs that appear in the writing of those who are well-adjusted—those who are generally referred to as "normal." It is hazardous to diagnose pathological symptoms unless you have had training in testing or treating mental patients. Handwriting contains some definite clues to both mental and physical ailments, but it is sometimes difficult to determine whether the mind influences the body or the body the mind.

A variety of t bars in one handwriting is the first definite sign of the neurotic. We say the writer has not one but *many* wills; he is in conflict; he is emotionally immature and irresponsible in some areas although he may be mature and responsible in others. The emotionally disturbed person's handwriting usually includes the t bar that does not go through the stem of the letter. The more these ineffectual t bars appear, the greater the guilt feelings, the more indecisive the person, and the more apt he is to live in the past.

All of us suffer guilt feelings to some extent, for as social beings we have consciences. The neurotic (or psychotic) reveals in this one sign the *degree* of guilt he feels. There are, of course, other corroborating signs. What we are primarily interested in is whether the guilt experienced by the writer allows him to live in peace with himself and others, or whether his behavior pattern is one of self-destructiveness or danger to others.

We can best explain the extent and type of an individual's emotional disturbance by observing the neurotic symptoms in his own handwriting, but it is always of enormous help to see handwriting specimens of his parents, or the person who represents the authority figure in his life.

Many handwritings of emotionally disturbed people reflect hope of recovery, and examining them we too can hope for a less anxiety-ridden world in the future.

The handwriting of a person going through the flux of change and chaos is bound to look chaotic. Even the great Sigmund Freud, as his handwriting in later life shows, reflected the confusion of his time. Perhaps because of his serious physical illness, the neurosis which led him to discover psychoanalysis became extreme as he realized his doom was sealed. His handwriting when he was younger is discussed on page 176. Here let us examine a specimen written when he was 72 years old, seriously ill, disillusioned and full of anger (Specimen 118).

We see first that the writing is angular and slanting to the right, and we conclude that Freud was a man of keen intellect with a leaning toward people. Noticeable also are the hooks at the end of words, and we see a man of tenacious drive and optimism—in spite of his anger and confusion. The signature with a small f puzzles us, for we know that he was no "shrinking violet." Was this attempt to appear humble an affectation? Or, at this time of his life, was it that he really didn't care what others thought of him? And look at the whip-like ending in the last stroke. This has been called a sadistic sign. He was angry at— shall we call it the Fates?—for having victimized him with an incurable disease. He became more self-centered (loops running into the line below), but his insatiable curiosity led him into exploring new and occult fields, quite out of keeping with his former explorations. Perhaps he felt that the end was not far and he wondered about the very things which he had explained in terms of man's perpetuation of his ego.

Surely, if we had seen this handwriting without the signature, we might have readily described the writer as a madman. And it may be true, as Omar Khayyám says, that "A hair perhaps divides the false and true." It is often a thin barrier which separates the genius from the madman.

PROF. DR. FREUD

WIEN, IX., BERGGASSE 19.

12. 2. 1929

[handwritten letter in German cursive]

Sigm. Freud

SPECIMEN 118 (reduced)

a qain   for   i

Kindness, in

that you   wi

Paris   soon .

SPECIMEN 119

Specimen 119 looks unusual. It is pleasant to the eye. Letters are clear and legible, with i dots placed firmly over the letter. Intuition is apparent in the breaks between letters, and there is the indication of sound practical judgment too. We see signs of talent, but the writing is large and this means exhibitionism. The writer, a woman, concerns herself with putting on some kind of show. She does it by giving parties and surrounding herself with people of prestige and talent. It is a compromise she has made—this making an art of entertaining. She finds a measure of contentment in it. There is no conflict here. The person operates on an even keel, as the straight basic line shows. She is adjusted. She could have been an artist, a designer (the writing looks like a design and the broad r tells us she is visual). But instead, she uses her artistry to entertain on a lavish scale. The wide spaces between letters show a kind of generosity which expresses itself in gestures. It also reveals a personal magnetism, gracefulness, charm. Repressed though the writer is in some areas, as shown by the t bar close to the stem, she compensates by the wide sweeps of motion. A hint of the altruistic g tells us she is interested in giving to others, and she does give out an aura of pleasantness. Perhaps it is true, after all, that agreeableness is a talent that draws people together, and she has it in full measure. She functions happily and constructively.

The Religious Fanatic

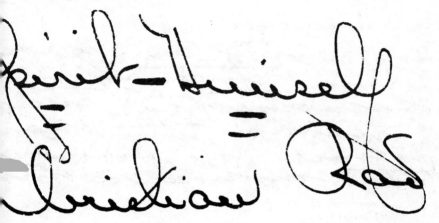

SPECIMEN 120

Specimen 120 is the handwriting of an emotional person who is visionary and extremely sensitive, as shown by the exaggerated wide upper loops. The Greek d reveals a cultured background. The writer finds in religion a world which represents the stage on which she is the leading lady and God is her leading man. One of the clues to her aberration is in the underscoring when referring to the authority figure in her life. Her world of fantasy is so rich that it is cloying, but she lives in it and describes it as flooded with "Christian Radiance." Everything she does is with a lavish hand. She lives alone surrounded by religious figures which she vivifies until they come alive to her. She talks to them and feels they understand her where other human beings do not.

Here is a person, then, who lives in a world of private meanings, yet there is sufficient exhibitionism (shown by the large writing) to seek contact with the outside world, and she does this by writing letters and poetry which she sends to various publications. The vertical angle of the writing tells us she feels she is the "preferred one" and because she is selective, she sees herself as the one selected to carry a spiritual message to others. She does this with charm and grace, for her writing is rounded, almost childlike in a sense, and although her emotions are pliable, her perceptions are not dulled. Everything she thinks of takes on a brightly colored aura, and her world of fantasy is the world she lives in.

The Compulsive-Obsessive

SPECIMEN 121

Specimen 121 is a classic example of the compulsive-obsessive person's handwriting. There is a tremendous drive, shown in t bars which are long most of the time and corroborated by finals which have a hook on the end. The writer seems to be driven to activity, even when there is no necessity for it, by something too strong for his reason to cope with. The lower loops running into the line below tell us of his strong sexual drive which is confirmed by the heavy pen pressure. They also reveal that he is self-centered and confused. Leaning to the right, the angle shows a great need for people, and those for whom he forms attachments become victims of his possessiveness until they feel they must get away from him or be stifled. This writer can be dangerous, indicated by the pen pressure that grows heavier at the end of a horizontal stroke (see the word "silly"). (In fact it finally became advisable for him to be institutionalized after attempted violence directed against someone he had been following for days and nights.) There is no apparent insight disclosed here since the letters in the words are all connected, and this tells us that he had no awareness of why he acted so compulsively.

The Sex Pervert

Added impetus was given the efforts in Washington ational foundation for the psychiatric treat coholics with the announcement today of

SPECIMEN 122

Specimen 122 belongs to a man in his late 60's who had been imprisoned for attacking young girls. (He had been a skilled watchmaker in a foreign country.) We see his sensuality in the heavy downstrokes of his letters. His paternalism—in this instance perverted—is indicated by the old-fashioned capital A. There is evidence of secretiveness in the "covering up" of the word "today" by the t bar in the preceding word. His history disclosed that he preferred the night, and in the darkness followed a little girl and coerced her into his furnished room. The pen pressure looks *pasty*, which is usually a sign of unstable emotions and sensuality. The intuition revealed by the breaks took the form of furtiveness as he sought to select his victim. Repressed, narrow-minded, living in a closed-in world, he had been a bachelor, physically unattractive to women in his own age group. Because he had the emotional make-up of a young boy, he chose young girls. At the same time, this satisfied his need to feel superior and he exerted a form of sadism upon them so he could feel powerful. Because he was fearful of expressing his own thoughts and feelings to a clinician (just as he was secretive with the prison authorities), he copied something when he wrote this specimen. But in talking of the reasons for his imprisonment, he sensed that the interrogator was not sitting in judgment on him and spoke frankly.

The Paranoiac

Specimen 123 was written in a mental institution. This handwriting belongs to a young woman whose disorientation in time and place, coupled with suspicions that "they" were plotting against her, caused

165

SPECIMEN 123

her to be placed where she could have custodial care. The wide spacing between words, and within words as well, is a major clue to her illness. Capitals appear in words where they do not belong—"any," "am." The broad r in "resting" both times is a clue to her saying that she *saw* people climbing into her window to take movies of her. In these words, too, the slurred endings tell of her evasiveness, while the exaggerated final on the last word corroborates our conclusion of her exaggerated suspicion. The entire writing *looks* peculiar, but because the lines are well spaced on the page, with margins on both sides, we may say that "there is a method to her madness."

The Drug Addict

Specimen 124, leaning far to the right, belongs to a hysterical person whose compulsiveness took the form of drug addiction. We see here signs of confusion coupled with the double-looped y which tell us the writer persisted in a drive over which she seemed to have lost control. Indeed, the t bars are lighter than the rest of the writing, showing their

166

SPECIMEN 124

ineffectualness. The swirl or first stroke on the capital M, two times, is a clue to secretiveness while the occasional darkening of the pen pressure gives us another clue to emotional instability. The writer was in an institution when this was written, and because she felt secure within its walls, her writing showed an upward swing of the basic line. Although the writing appears to be open because of the natural flow, close examination will reveal the slurring that indicates evasiveness in the word "in" in the last line. In addition, some of the letters in the word "practically" are so small that they are out of harmony with other, more clearly executed ones. Only one i is dotted, and we may conclude that the writer has many blind spots, closing her eyes to that which she does not wish to see.

She remains today an unreconstructed drug addict, and because she is a nurse, she uses her profession to cater to her aberration. She functions only long enough to amass the drugs to which she has access, builds up reasons why she should leave the job, and then goes on a drug spree.

The Victim of a Heart Attack

The writer of Specimen 125 was on a trip and was fatally stricken in his hotel room. The bathroom tissue on which the specimen was written matched that in the bathroom of his room. It was found on his person and was the only written document left by the deceased.

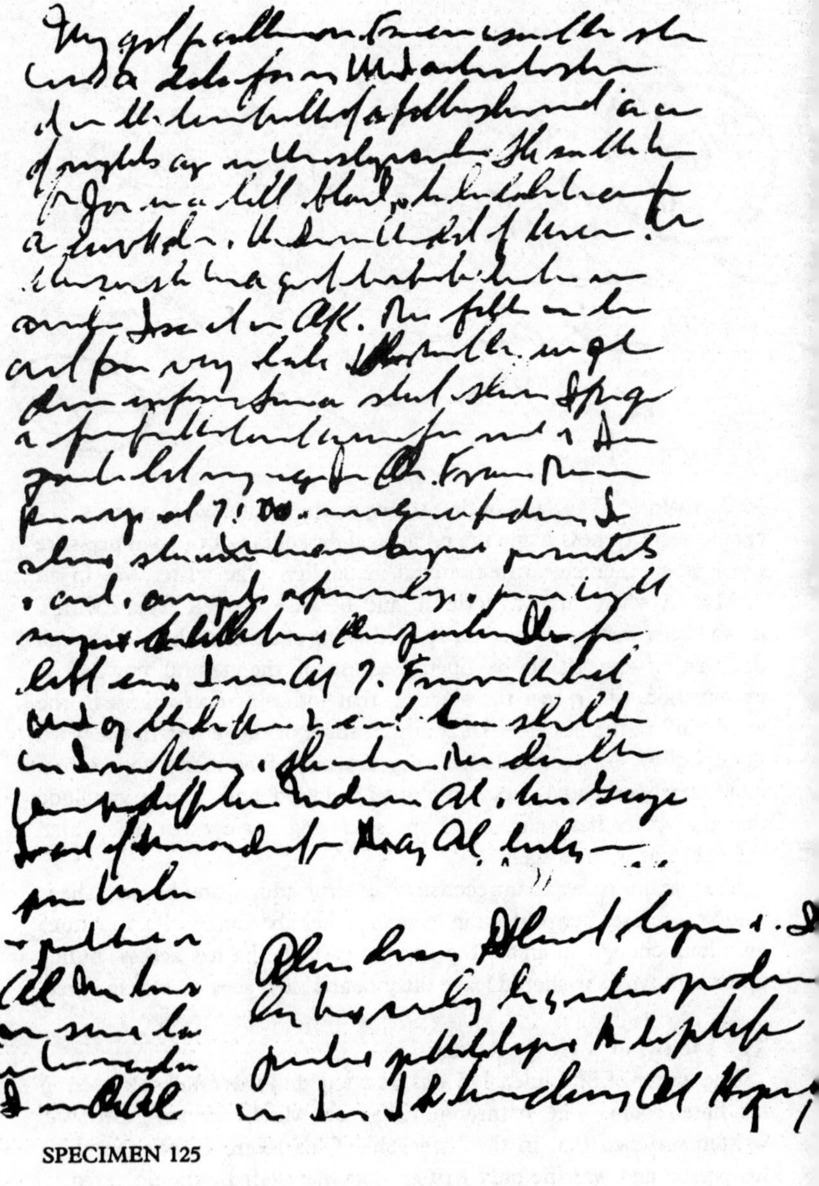

SPECIMEN 125

SPECIMEN 125
(enlarged)

Only part of the message is reproduced here. As you can see, it is practically indecipherable. The first two words, closely examined, appear to be "My God," almost as though the man, in deep pain, was saying a prayer. (A specimen of his handwriting written earlier, when he was ostensibly in good health, disclosed strong religious leanings and the fact that he was unhappy in his work as a travelling salesman. He would have been happier in a religious vocation.)

We are here concerned with his last message written on the only paper available at the time the heart attack convulsed him. His will to live must have been strong, for he wrote on two and a half sheets. We can only conjecture that, as a religious man, he was making his last covenant with God.

The specimen, blown up photostatically, contains one consistent sign that gives us the clue to his heart condition. This sign is in the *breaks* that appear in the upper loops consistently. The breaks show clearly in both the negative of the photostat and in the blow-ups. The pen marks are those of a man struggling during a heart attack. It is not improbable that the pain became so intense that he reached for his medication in the bathroom and took an overdose. (This is conjecture.) His first name was Albert and we seem to recognize a reference to the name in a number of places. It is interesting, too, that he kept a fairly straight margin on the left side of the tissue, telling us that he still had an aesthetic awareness even though his mind seemed to have become blurred like a picture taken out of focus.

Since broken (or ragged) upper loops indicate a heart condition, it would be well to keep a wary eye on upper loops in all specimens of handwriting. If a break appears once, it may be due to a faulty pen, but if there are many, it is time for a thorough physical examination which may avert a heart attack.

Partial Eyesight

We know when we observe Specimen 126 that something is wrong, but we also see that the person functions despite his disability—we notice signs of self-discipline in the bowed t bars, some of them with a tenacious hook on the end. The mind thinks quickly, and the rhythm isn't essentially disturbed. But the writer has the need to go over his letters because he does not see them clearly. His impulse is to communicate with others, as shown by the right slant, but his impairment

SPECIMEN 126

has caused him to resort to shrewdness so that other people will not be aware of the extent of his visual handicap. He is an inventive person, shown by the constructed capital A, and in the first word, fifth line, there is a printed small s telling us he has talent. We may conclude that he has come to terms with his deficient eyesight and is functioning in a constructive capacity. The small closed b in the word "best," in the sixth line, reveals his business sense, and he uses it in connection with one of his inventions which he has marketed. The *going over* of strokes in any handwriting means compulsiveness, and in an individual with visual limitations it seems natural that he should have become compulsive in order to make himself understood.

Polio Victim

The woman who wrote Specimen 127 was operated on many times to straighten out her leg so she could walk, although she does so with a limp. The jerky rhythm in this specimen represents the stiffness with which she uses her lower limbs. The strong will, indicated in firm t bars, tells us of her will to live and courage in the face of the surgical trials she experienced. The square formation of the y in the last word corroborates the obstinacy with which she hangs on, despite many obstacles. She is now close to middle age, yet there seems something

171

ings. I have left Howard Beach last December and now I am with Mother and Cécile's home will stay

childlike about the writing, as in the rounded formation of the letter m. Because her life has been so filled with pain, she finds escape from this world in a world of fantasy, shown in her upper loops. That many of them are compressed is to be expected, since her spinsterhood has permitted no emotional outlet. She finds expression in the use of her hands and an anchor in her religion which provides an area of strength. She has learned to live with her disability without feeling sorry for herself. Some of her blunt finals tell us she can be obstinate about having her own way, but since there is also a positive strength indicated, we may assume that she functions on an adjusted, useful level, taking her unfortunate experiences in her stride, jerky though it is.

Brain Tumor

Just as the woman who wrote Specimen 128 remains in a wheel chair because of paralysis from two brain tumors, she writes on lines which offer her a balance to express herself. It is an exceptional case since there are no similar case histories upon which to base a prognosis. The writer has shown unusual courage in trying to adjust to her life in a city hospital. Although there is a need for open self-expression, as shown in the open capital D and small a's and o's, she is nevertheless often taciturn with those around her. This is because of paranoid trends, shown in wide spacing between words, which increased during

Dearest Nadya

I wrote this ma

but had no envelop

Love, W

her stay in the hospital, although they were a part of her behavior pattern before it. The writing has become more rounded than it was before her surgical experiences. She is in the position of a helpless child for whom everything has to be done and her emotional structure is one of regression to the infantile level. Nevertheless, she is unusually alert for someone so stricken. The printed L in the word "Love" tells us there remains a residue of constructive ability which gives her the will to live and to build, out of her shattered life, something to fill the time she spends in an institution. Furthermore, she feels secure within its walls, and this has added to her calm and capacity to communicate with her friends in the world outside of her confined one.

Ann Rutledge

It is interesting to note how the handwriting of Ann Rutledge (Specimen 129), who is often referred to as the "love of Lincoln's life," shows an ebbing and flowing of her energy. Here the consistent disconnecting of words has the connotation of illness. She was always in delicate health and died of "brain fever." Often, as the end of life approaches, an individual's intuition becomes sharpened. Here it appears that Ann's writing "gasps" almost as she might have done

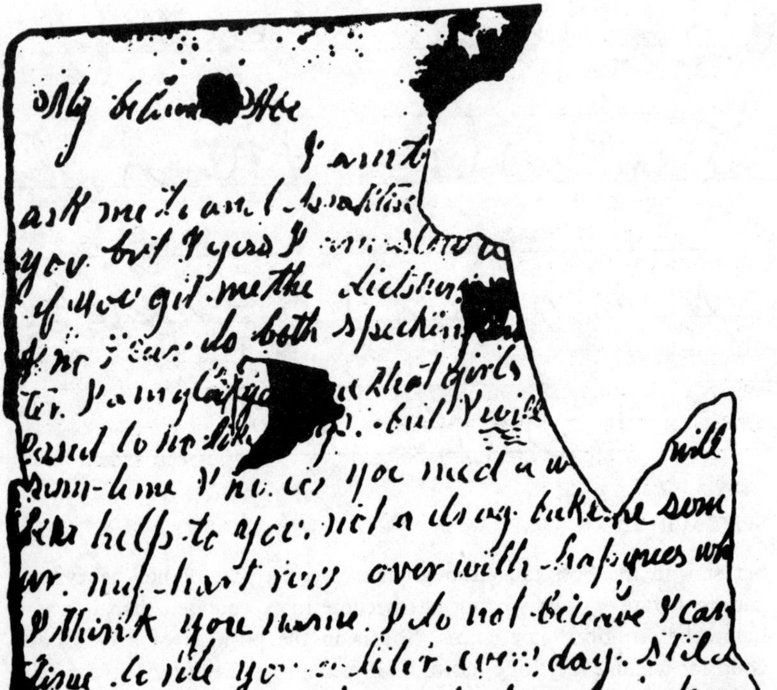

SPECIMEN 129 **(reduced)**

during this period of her illness. We see first the old-fashioned formation of the capital M consistent with the protective A in her signature. These are formations common to the period in which this was written. Despite the poor spelling, Ann's writing reveals "mental formations"—the small b in the salutation "beloved" (my beloved Abe); then again in h's all through the writing, although in this she is not consistent. The t bars vary—most of them are ineffectual and do not go through the stem, showing a typical feminine passivity. Yet here is another connotation: with the ebbing of her strength, the will too became weaker. But Ann was not really a weak individual, and you will notice a few strong t bars: "the" in the fourth line, "both" in the fifth line, "tole" in the fourteenth line, and three lines below that, in the first word, "the," the t bar is *above* the stem, strong, firm and showing her vivid imagination, spirit of adventure and romanticism. A great deal more can be said about Ann. Perhaps you will be able to see much more than is written in this ostensibly simple letter to a great and simple man!

23. Genius -- In What Does It Consist?

Men are great as they are kind.—EMERSON

Many people have tried to define the word genius and have come up with different answers. It is my feeling that when a person leaves a legacy of some kind—great books, great paintings, theories which are workable for the good of mankind—we may refer to him as a genius. Our concern here is not to ascertain whether or not men and women living today possess genius, but rather to examine the handwritings of those who have influenced our culture and added to our emotional and intellectual growth. What is the common denominator? We shall see.

Surely Sigmund Freud has had enormous influence on 20th century society. We will start with an analysis of his handwriting when he was young, and see what it reveals. Compare it to the specimen on page 161, written 47 years later.

Sigmund Freud

Specimen 130 is the letter in which Freud proposed marriage to the woman who became his wife. It was written when he was 26 years old. It may be difficult to believe that the man who dealt so frankly with the primitive sexual urges of human beings was himself something of a prude! We view this in his capital M, the old-fashioned formation which means adherence to conventional forms as well as a paternal, protective instinct. To be sure, he wooed and won Martha Bernays with an ardor filled with jealousy, unreasonable demands, a passion bordering on frenzy, at times. Yet much of his wooing was done in writing, and he spent more time speaking of love than making love.

Within him was a terrific struggle between the dictates of turbulent emotions and a mind which could be clear and scientific in its reasoning. We see some rather long t bars revealing his drive and determination,

Jacob Freud
WIEN.

Wien, den 15 Juni 1882

My sweet darling girl

Ich weiss noch nicht, wie ich diese Zeilen
vor die Augen des theuren Mädchens
bringen werde; ich glaube, ich werde eine
Petition der Schwestern an Eli veranstalten
um unsere Begegnung am Samstag zu
sichern u. diesen verwegenen Brief einschmuggeln
... lassen, bevor ich es mir aufschreibe
theure Martha zu schreiben, dass ich in den
wenigen Minuten, die uns gehören werden,
nicht Muth u. vielleicht nicht Fassung finden
werde, alles gut Ihnen zu bekennen; die
kleinen Intriguen u. die rücksichtslosen Ent-
würfe, welche Ihre Abwesenheit in Hamburg
erfordert. Theure Martha wie haben
Sie mein Leben verändert. Es war so
so wunderbar schön in Ihrem Hause,
in Ihrer Nähe, aber es verbitterte
mir die wenigen Momente, in welchen Eli
uns allein liess, das meine eigensüchtigen
Absichten zu vermerken, es wäre mir wie eine
Verletzung der herzlich gebotenen Gast-
freundschaft erschienen; in Marthas Nähe
wollte ich nicht unedler thun. Diesen
Abend u. deinen Spaziergang hätte ich

SPECIMEN 130

and in his own words he was "tenacious and active." But he was also full of self-doubt as evidenced in some t bars which do not go through the stem of the letter (look at the specimen under a magnifying glass). Yet he could be aggressive in a querulous way, besieged by changing moods, some of which bordered on a temporary feeling of hopelessness. (This is evident in the word that hangs over on the end of the sixth line.)

His angular formations tell us that he could be exacting, demanding, efficient; that he was an extremist who hated half-measures; that he drove himself and did things the hard way; that he was relentless in probing the truth to the bitter end, and this is what made him a great scientist. But he could be submissive when his emotions became involved, and he revealed a tenderness as sincere as his outbursts of fury.

Notice the altruistic g in the word "girl" in the salutation. This, in combination with the t bar which did not go through the stem, gives us clues to his occasional feelings of martyrdom, his masochism and his frequent feeling of being misunderstood. He fought against this as against his primitive impulses, but because of a need to make his contribution, he persisted in the face of opposition, criticism and feelings of rejection. He was essentially a reformer, a healer, an intensely social-minded being.

His intuition, revealed in the breaks between letters all through the writing, was uncanny, and he was forever analyzing motives, gestures, happenings—even during the most fervent period of his courtship. It was then that he ran through the whole gamut of emotions from ecstasy to despair, yet at the same time he could be calm, detached and coldly scientific in his work. Perhaps this is the combination that might be considered the essential feature of any great genius! Surely, Freud had it in full measure. His excellent memory persisted even in his latter years, when his handwriting began to show signs of dis-integration.

Michelangelo

In the handwriting of Michelangelo, sculptor, painter, architect and poet, we are struck at a glance with so many original formations. Specimen 131 is in Italian but its originality speaks a universal language.

SPECIMEN 131

Look at the unusual way he forms his small c in the word "chromo" (first line) and in other words where a "ch" appears.

Intuition, without which the artist could not create, is shown all through the writing in breaks between letters. Pen pressure is uniformly heavy, telling us of his sensuousness to forms, colors, music. Even in the foreign language, we see a small g resembling the number 8 and we know, by now, that this is the "literary g." This is corroborated in Michelangelo's handwriting by the Greek d. We know that he wrote sonnets and poems, and his paintings, too, told a story. He had many ways of communicating his thoughts, genius that he was.

179

Notice especially the capital V form in his signature—the arrow pointing upward on the first stroke and the hook on the final upward stroke. The former indicates his aspiration toward "the heavens"; the latter shows his tenacity of purpose, the kind of persistence characteristic of the genius. And look at the small printed s's all through the writing. There are some bowed t's too, revealing his self-discipline arising from spirituality. The other t bars over the stem we have come to recognize as the sign of a vivid imagination, perfectionism, a rich world of fantasy. The writing from a distance looks like a design in which rhythm is evident among unusual forms and structure. His attention to detail is plainly seen in the word "puro" in the fifth line. There is a kind of order, though not of the precise kind. Perhaps some of the unusual strokes give a hint of a quality of inner madness, held in check and disciplined. To quote Stephen Spender, "The difference between art and madness . . . is this: the artist projects and re-creates outside himself a world of ideas which he puts in order: the madman *is* a world of disordered ideas."

Fyodor Dostoevsky

What in the handwriting of one of Russia's outstanding writers (if not the greatest) gives us the clues to his genius? Examining Specimen 132, we see signs of culture, great sensitivity (in the light pen pressure), small writing showing powers of concentration and the altruistic sign telling us of his great interest in people. He signed twice, each time differently, telling us of a number of facets to his personality. His open capital D reveals his openheartedness and generosity, and we think of Emerson's words: "Men are great as they are kind."

The breaks between letters tell us of his keen intuition and insight, and the high i dots reveal imagination. Some of his finals rise upward, and these combined with the light pen pressure reveal his spirituality. The pen pressure darkens in spots and we might construe this as a clue to emotional changes taking place in him, often unexpectedly. To the advanced student in graphology this is a clue to his epilepsy, while to the amateur it might be puzzling. See his underscore and remember that it means compensation for an inferiority complex. Those who are familiar with his life know that he had periods when he felt quite inadequate. He was prolific in his writing for two reasons: he was a born scribbler and had to write to express himself, and since he was

меня, а ты завтра зайди ко мнѣ непремѣнно обѣщала. До свидания милый другъ, обнимаю и поздравляю тебя

Тебя безконечно любящій
И въ тебя безконечно вѣрующій
твой весь
Ѳ. Достоевскій

Ты мое будущее все — и надежда и вѣра и счастіе и блаженство — все. —

paid by the page, he often wrote uncorrected copy and submitted it in order to pay the gambling debts he had incurred.

Even though his writing is in Russian, it reveals a supersensitive, impressionable, imaginative individual with a rich fantasy world. Nevertheless, he keenly observed the reality around him and expressed it masterfully in his novels.

Specimen 133, called "Fantasy Notes," is written in an almost microscopic hand. Examined under a magnifying glass it shows neurotic signs in the t bar which is on the left of the stem, other strokes not found in copybooks and embellished capitals. There are t bars

FANTASY NOTES

SPECIMEN 133

above the stem of the letters, too, and many of the same signs we observed in the first specimen. We know that Dostoevsky had a capacity for hard work, in spite of periods of indecision and procrastination, when we see the long t bar in the last word of this document.

Dostoevsky was not in reality the meek, self-effacing Prince Myshkin of the largely autobiographical "The Idiot." Rather his self-effacing manner was a façade which covered up an enormous residue of rage, and it was this rage which took the form of an epileptic seizure when it spilled over.

If we study Dostoevsky's writings, as well as his handwriting, we are forced to conclude that he "foamed at the mouth" at injustice of any kind. From his early childhood he must have had intense feelings of rejection which later latched on to his rage against injustice. As an adult, he experienced an empathy toward those human beings upon whom society had imposed injustices. We might go so far as to say that his epileptic convulsions were tantamount to "blowing his top." And if we are to consider the upper zones, we see him as *headless!*

In "The Idiot" he graphically describes his feelings just before his fury reached a racing boil, at which point a seizure took over.

> Then suddenly something seemed torn asunder from him; his soul was flooded with intense *inner* light. The moment lasted perhaps half a second, yet he clearly and consciously remembered the beginning, the first sound of the fearful scream which broke of itself from his breast and which he could not have checked by any effort. Then his consciousness was instantly extinguished and complete darkness followed.

Charles Lamb

The most noticeable feature in Charles Lamb's handwriting (Specimen 134) is the falling down lines, and we know from this that he had terrific periods of depression and unhappiness. The psychiatrist would categorize him as a manic-depressive, and his history reveals information to substantiate this diagnosis. He had been institutionalized a number of times for his illness. At the same time, we are impressed with the perfectly straight margin on the left and with the fact that the lines—though they fall down like the branches of the weeping willow—are still clear and without signs of confusion. How do we reconcile this with his emotional illness, except to describe him as having a method to his madness! His aesthetic sense conditioned many of his appetites,

183

I had sense in dreams of a Beauty rare,
Whom fate had spell-bound, and rooted there.
Stooping like some enchanted theme,
Over the marge of that chrystal stream
Where the blooming Greek, to Echo blind,
With self love fond had to waters joined,
Ages had waked, and ages slept,
And that bending posture still she kept.
For her eyes she may not turn away,
Till a fairer object shall pass that way;
Till an image more beauteous this world can show,
Than her own which she sees in the mirror below.
Pore on, fair Creature, for ever pore,
Nor dream to be disenchanted more,
For vain is expedance, and wish is vain,
Till a new Narissus can come again.

Chs Lamb.

SPECIMEN 134

and even in his deepest unhappiness he could still react to beauty, whether in the form of a flower, a child, or the cadence of music. The capital N in the third line from the bottom gives us the clue to his paternalism, and this was seen in the protective attitude he had toward his sister who was even sicker than he was and very dependent upon him.

184

Paris 7 Mars 1888

Verehrter Herr Berger!
Ich komme in London
am 19ten an und werde
im Hotel Dieudonné, wie
Sie mir es geraten haben
absteigen.
Die Violinsolo partie (sie
ist im 1ten Geigen partie
gedruckt) schicke ich Ihnen
heute. Auf baldigen
Wiedersehen.
Ihr ergebener
P. Tschaïkowsky

Piotr Ilich Tchaikovsky

Written in German, Tchaikovsky's handwriting (Specimen 135) shows, at a glance, the sign of anxiety, in the first word of the body of the letter (Ich). We see signs of intuition in the breaks between letters and the strong t bars show a capacity for self-discipline and consistent hard work. (This seems to be the common denominator of all the geniuses whose handwritings I have analyzed.) And we observe the confusion which sometimes assailed him when he became subjective and self-condemning. We see further the same signs that appear in many a genius's hand: altruism, imagination, a careful memory. (When he did dot his i's they were close to the letter; when they remained undotted, it was because he chose to forget that which was to him most painful.) The high upper loops give us the clue to the world of fantasy without which he could not have composed the music we now enjoy. ("The Nutcracker Suite" is pure fantasy.) It is an emotional rather than an intellectual hand, and indeed his emotions governed him much more than his reasoning, though he could think clearly and logically many times. It is, in fact, known that he began as a lawyer but abandoned this profession to devote himself to his music.

WALT WHITMAN

SPECIMEN 136

186

Walt Whitman

Walt Whitman speaks of "divine things" and we notice, in Specimen 136, a consistent t bar which is bowed—the *sign of heaven*. His handwriting slants to the right, with the sign of altruism, and we know of his love for people, while the breaks for intuition tell us of his keen insight into their motivations. His Greek d veers to the left in the last stroke and it is a clue to concern with self—he identified himself with his own sex, often preferring to be with men. His paternalism is revealed in the old-fashioned capital N in the word "Nature," and we know he had a protective attitude toward the weak, the downtrodden, the underdog. He was a real humanitarian, and his rhythmic writing gives us the clue to the poet, the music in his soul which he expressed in words. Notice that the signature is larger than the rest of his writing, and from this we conclude that he had an awareness of his own importance; that he felt the power he could exert over others. Yet the sign of self-discipline (which you have probably come to recognize by now), tells us that he held himself in leash and used his power where he felt it would do the most good.

Thomas Wolfe

What impresses us in the handwriting of Thomas Wolfe (Specimen 137) is his almost unbridled energy, almost like a wild race horse charging ahead with some fury. Yet there *is* a sign of control, caution, reserve—a holding back. The uneven pen pressure gives us a clue to changes in emotional tempo; the dark marks indicate his sensuousness. Some of his t bars show his rebelliousness, sarcasm, compulsive drive, while others reveal his tenacity of purpose, and still others show the kind of inertia that comes on the heels of inner turmoil and mixed feelings. Many blunt finals in the writing are certainly a clue to his sadism, his bitterness toward a world which he felt did not really understand him, though his effort to communicate with it through his books was prodigious. He wrote obsessively about himself, his life and family, as though he were making a bid for acceptance and understanding.

This was no altruist, and it makes us wonder whether he gave because he was impelled to make a contribution, or whether he had to write to give vent to his anger. Did he make a bid for the sympathy of others, or write because he was "possessed" by his need to do so?

& he said "Decidedly." I asked him what changes and revisions he thought should be made & he said he did not know that there were any — it is simply not the kind of Trust Company, Place de la Concorde, Paris.

With love, & the very best wishes to all,

Tom Wolfe

Thomas Wolfe never broke the natal cord which bound him to his mother and his past. Most of his work, as we know, is autobiographical and perhaps in this lies his limitation—just as his handwriting, despite signs of talent, imagination, an almost adolescent naiveté, is significant because of the few signs of intuition! His interest in other people was less evident than his interest in himself. Yet his handwriting shows no appreciable insight into either others or himself. So many undotted i's tell us of the many blind spots he had and of his subjective reasoning, while the slurring of letters (as in the words "any," "Company," "kind") indicates that although he wrote with apparent frankness, there was much about which he was evasive. Is Thomas Wolfe's handwriting that of the person with the strength of the consecrated who withholds nothing of himself—the real genius? It poses the question of whether this writer will be counted in the ranks of the great. Will his work live after those who identify with him are no longer here to appreciate him, or will his outpourings become something of the past?

Edna St. Vincent Millay

Edna St. Vincent Millay was introverted, highly imaginative and living in a rich world of fantasy, as her t bars consistently show, yet her handwriting (Specimen 138) presents to us a picture of a realist, nevertheless, since the writing is in a vertical angle. ("And why should I be cold, my lad, and why should you repine?") She gives the impression of being cold, detached and impersonal. (She did not mix very much with other people and lived alone at the time of her death.) The emotion she felt was generated into thought and she was often the philosopher, the scientist, more than the emotionally charged artist and poet. There are signs of intuition in breaks between letters. Slurs which are no letters at all tell us she did not reveal herself to the world except through her poetry. The signs of introversion are augmented by backward strokes in the words "will not" and in her signature. She observed her own reactions and put them into poetic or dramatic form. The hint of an altruistic turn in the last stroke on the y in her name tells us that she had the instinct to make her contribution. And it is here that we see the possibility that because of her giving, her poetry may live.

[handwritten letter]

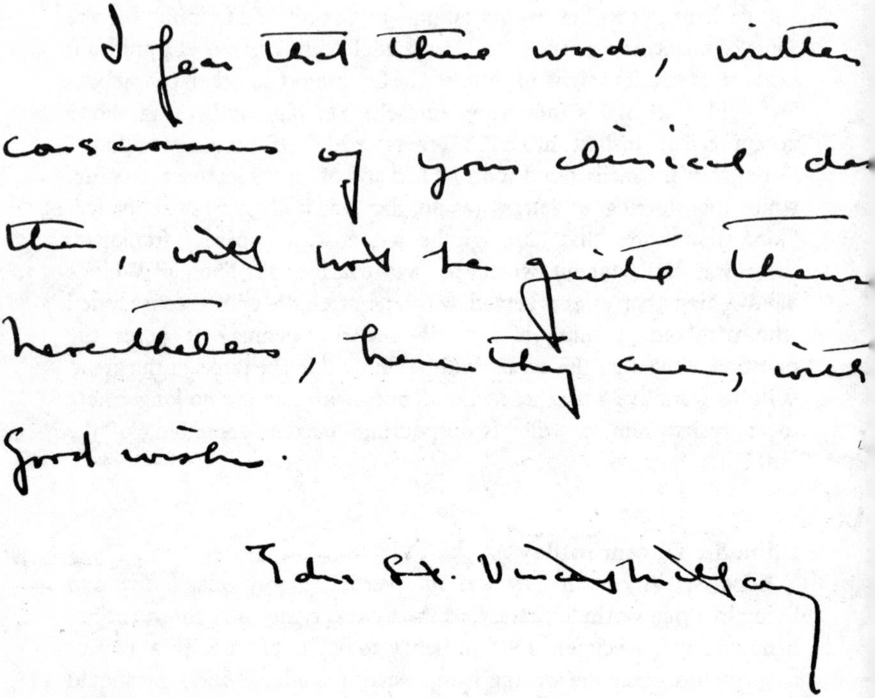

I fear that these words, written consciously of your clinical ... them, will not be quite them nevertheless, here they are, with good wishes.

Edna St. Vincent Millay

SPECIMEN 138

Willa Cather

The small vertical writing of Willa Cather (Specimen 139) tells us she was a realist, but also a person of vivid imagination, as shown in the consistently high t bars. Her capital I, made like a Roman numeral, expresses severity in some of her tastes; intuition, as shown in the breaks between letters, confirms what we know from her writings—that she had a keen insight into people. All through the specimen we see consistent signs of altruism. We feel, for this reason (and others), that her work will live. The slurs made many times in the place of letters tell us that there was much about her personal life she preferred not to reveal; she made herself understood through her books. Her

March 21ˢᵗ

My Dear Miss Colganora:

I am sailing on Saturday and have not time to reply to your letter as I would like to do. I can only tell you that it will ask Zoë Akins, a friend of Miss Kennia, to bring you to see some hypnosis, and can tell me why this story touched you so much.

Cordially yours

Willa Cather

frankness shows in her capital D and O. See the small d in the word "Cordially" and also in the body of the specimen, and remember what we said before: that it shows reticence. In her personal life, she was often detached, quiet, unreachable. We see the signs of the literary figure in the g made like number 8, in the small writing which shows powers of concentration, and in the mental formations throughout. Willa Cather was an astute observer of life. She thought for a long time about an experience before she could write about it. We may also construe the small capitals in the salutation of this letter as signs of modesty, although those in her simple signature are somewhat larger. This tells us that hers was a healthy ego; she neither overestimated nor underestimated herself. Rather she accepted herself with a calm detachment which did not reveal the turbulent emotions she sometimes felt.

MADAME CURIE

Madame Curie

Madame Curie's handwriting, Specimen 140, is written in Polish. The well-spaced lines still reveal the writer's well-organized thinking. Here is the Greek d and the spiritual t bar telling us of her lofty motives and ability to keep a tight lid on her emotions. We notice also signs of sound practical judgment in the single downstroke of the y and g formations. We know this stroke means mathematical ability too. But how are we to judge the uneven pen pressure in a hand that is distinguished by its simplicity? We may say she had changeable feelings attended by mild confusion, possibly because she was torn between her work which absorbed her so much, and her duties as a mother. By an organized effort, she managed to take care of both, although they sometimes got her down. This is shown in the falling down of words at the end of some lines. The wide spacing between her words gives us a clue to a kind of paranoid fear, perhaps that others might not understand her dual status of woman and scientist. Her simple, rounded signature tells us she was fundamentally a gentle person, while the large capitals reveal her taste, dignity and pride.

Albert Einstein

Small letters, light pen pressure and simple formations in Professor Einstein's handwriting (Specimen 141) tell us he was an extremely sensitive man, modest and retiring, with many of the elements of the hermit-introvert. Capital letters are small. The A in his signature is a simplification of the old-fashioned formation, and tells us of his protective attitude toward the underprivileged and downtrodden. His prodigious memory is revealed in the careful dotting of his i's. The margins on both sides, coupled with clearly defined lines, indicate an aesthetic nature which made demands of him in a simple, unpretentious way. The rhythmic writing itself, and the graceful final in the last word of the seventh line, are clues to his musical ability, while the t bar above the stem in his last name tells a story all its own. Here we have the clue to his world of fantasy, imagination, spirituality, and his desire to work for the good of humanity. He often curbed his personal desires to achieve his dreams. We may assume, therefore, that the destruction resulting from his scientific discoveries had a crushing effect upon him and contributed to his moods of depression. This depression is revealed in words which fall slightly over even though

Sehr geehrte Frau Olyanova!

Ich hätte Ihre Bitte gewiss früher erfüllt, wenn Ihre Briefe nicht in der Fülle ihrer Geschwister aus meinem Blickfeld verschwunden wären. Denn Graphologie hat mich stets interessiert, wenn ich mich auch nie systematisch dafür interessiert habe; ich mache es mit Schriften wie mit Gesichtern, ich urteile instinktiv.

Hochachtungsvoll

A. Einstein.

SPECIMEN 141

the basic line rises upward, revealing his underlying optimism. Perhaps in his simplicity lay the seed of his greatness, although he himself minimized it. Often he felt small and unworthy, and like most geniuses he felt isolated and alone. The capital D in the fifth line gives us a clue to a kind of mild frivolity in his make-up, and this took the form of childlike indulgences in pleasures out of doors and close to Nature.

Lloyd C. Douglas

Lloyd Douglas's handwriting (Specimen 142) shows the vivid imagination in the t bars above the stem. Here too is the small printed s and the sign of altruism. It is an outgoing hand leaning to the right, with breaks between letters showing intuition. His interest in people

This village is so apathetic that they have stopped ringing a curfew because it woke the people up. All the under-statement in this letter may be explained my environment.

Lloyd C Douglas

SPECIMEN 142

was an absorbing one. He had keen insights into their motivations and emphasized the good, the spiritual. Some anxiety is indicated in the patching up of letters in the word "village," but this is not surprising when we learn that the letter from which this fragment was taken was written when he was visiting his dying mother.

It is known that Lloyd Douglas was a minister at one time, and the stage presence he needed for appearances in the pulpit reveals itself in the underscore of his signature. Indeed, he had a strong sense of drama. He compensated for the inferiority complex that had its seat in his early childhood by becoming a popular novelist. We know of his religious bent through his novels "The Robe" and "The Big Fisherman." Except for the lower loop in his signature which has a healthy swing, others are either insignificant or made with a rightward turn, and we conclude that his literary expressions were the result of an impelling force. (It was an accident that he became wealthy because of his writings.) As he had once preached sermons with enthusiasm, so he wrote his novels. He achieved monetary success because his works filled a spiritual need in such a large number of people. Perhaps for this reason, his books may outlive many more erudite volumes.

JAMES HILTON

" When you are getting on in years (but not ill, of course), you get very sleepy at times, and the hours seem to pass like lazy cattle moving across a landscape."

James Hilton

Goodbye Mr Chips

James Hilton

The handwriting of James Hilton (Specimen 143) indicates that he may have achieved success less from a consistent drive than from spurts of enthusiasm, as revealed by the t bar which flies away from the stem. The vertical angle and the altruistic y tell us of his capacity to deal with people sympathetically yet realistically. (This angle is due to Anglo-Saxon influence, although the g made like number 8 also tells us he was able to adapt to foreign environments, as he did when he made his home in the United States.)

He was the observer, often detached in an impersonal way, reserved in that he did not readily reveal his own feelings unless it was through his writings—and his handwriting. And these were feelings of a sensitive nature, sifted through a mind that sat in judgment on his emotions. Those who could get close to him aroused his generosity, as shown in the open a's and o's, yet there was also a measure of caution (see the small a in his first name). Although a sense of the dramatic shows in the underscore, notice that it is under the name of his fictional character. We conclude from this that in his unconscious he identified with Mr. Chips, and revealed something of himself in his literary character. The margin on the right grows larger, giving us a clue to an aesthetic sense which often overrode the practical in him. (If you examine this piece of writing under a magnifying glass, you may notice a tremulousness, especially in the words "across a landscape." This was written not long before he died, for he was much sicker than anyone suspected.)

Mary Baker Eddy

We see in Mrs. Eddy's handwriting (Specimen 144) the drive and capacity for hard work revealed by the long t crossings. The sign of altruism appears too. The pen pressure sometimes becomes extremely dark, especially in the underscoring of words. This is a sign of her fanatic emphasis of what she believed in. Other heavy strokes reveal her intense emotionality which sometimes took the form of bitterness —when she felt she was criticized or misunderstood. Extreme sensitivity amounting to touchiness is revealed by the uncrossed t which has a hook going upward at the end. The incurve on the word "that" (last word in the fourth line) is something often seen in the handwritings of religious people who spend time in reflection, even though the right slant may reveal definite extroversion. The capital O in the date of the

Lovingly ever thine

R + M B Eddy

Pleasant View.
Concord. N.H. *Oct. 3 1904*

My dearest Student

U sent to you a 20 dollar gold piece not as money, for that can neither express nor pay for your kindness in helping me outside as on appeal. It was time

SPECIMEN 144

letter also shows Mrs. Eddy's need for self-expression. This O, too, in combination with the black strokes, tells us she could be brutally frank! The extreme right slant of the writing expresses an ardor often amounting to hysteria, and in studying Mrs. Eddy's life the student of psychology will discover that it was this ardor that led her into a field which attracted great numbers of followers. The pragmatist accepts Mrs. Eddy as a figure in history whose theories, when put to use, have brought good results to many people.

ALFRED ADLER

DR. ALFRED ADLER
NERVENARZT
WIEN, I., DOMINIKANERBASTEI 10
TELEPHON 71-8-27
—

WIEN, am _13/VII 1926_

Dear friend,

much thanks for your friendly efforts. I

I accept the proposition of Dr Cr.-h and .

at the 7th November.

I hope to find there also other pupils

can spend nearly 14 days without a great

man from London I go to America alread

Adler.

SPECIMEN 145

199

Dr. Alfred Adler

Because Dr. Adler was not physically robust, his theory that many of our inadequacies arise from physical limitations bears some scrutiny. In Specimen 145, see in what a light pen pressure he writes! His small handwriting shows powers of concentration; he was a thinker with spiritual overtones, as shown by the bowed t bar in the first word of the last line. The second word in this line gives us a clue to the fact that he had periods of anxiety, as does the word "days" in the line above. Still, he seemed calm, was always friendly, and manifested much patience. His intuition, as revealed in so many breaks between the letters in words, was extreme, and he sensed a great deal about his patients by merely looking at them. (See the broad r which appears so often, even though he also formed the other one.) Although the Greek d appears in many places, we also see the d indicative of reticence ("days" and "already"). He was often reticent about his personal life in which he suffered much pain. Yet many of his small a's and o's are open at the top, as is the capital A in his signature, and we know that he could be prolific in his writings. There is no underscore in his signature, for Dr. Adler was a modest man whose personality was in harmony with his character. So many rounded formations tell us of his gentleness, while the old-fashioned capital N, although simplified—because he was a simple man—tells us he was paternalistic and interested in helping the sick, the downtrodden, the underdog. He was a family man and he placed emphasis on the family constellation.

24. Outstanding Personalities on the Contemporary Scene

Claudette Colbert

The handwriting of Claudette Colbert (Specimen 146) tells us she does everything quickly and with grace and rhythm. The t bar above the stem in the words "handwriting" and "the twentieth" gives us the clue to her vivid imagination, spirit of adventure, perfectionism. She does not dot her i's many times, mainly because details she considers unimportant often annoy her, but because there is so much intuition and i dots that are high above the letter, we conclude that she has a sensory memory and a recall of that which touches her emotions deeply. The hook on the end of the y in "cordially" tells us she "hangs on," and indeed she has—to her stardom!

Notice the extremely wide upper loop in her first name. What a rich world of fantasy she has! How fortunate that she has practical balance and a capacity for clear, logical reasoning, as shown by connected letters in many words and a tendency toward the vertical angle more often than any other. The pen pressure tends toward lightness with occasional heavy strokes, and we know from this that she can approach a situation with great sensitivity or give a dramatic moment emotional emphasis. The wide margin on the left—and the rest of the letter showed it growing wider—gives us a clue to an aesthetic sense which often overrides the practical. The underscored signature tells us further that she exudes magnetism, tempered by a measure of reserve when she first meets people. Optimistic, cheerful, bright and perceptive, she is also the essence of femininity.

Your autograph if our Dreadful fans want it — I am of mood Claudette Colbert Sunday — February the twelfth

SPECIMEN 146

Joan Crawford

The large, rightward-leaning handwriting of Joan Crawford (Specimen 147) tells us she does everything with a lavish and unstinting hand! She possesses a tremendous drive as shown in the long t bars coupled with connecting letters in all her words. But this means something else: she is amazingly logical, even though this fact sometimes gets her into difficulty because she does not trust the intuitive flashes she gets.

The lower loops—long, wide, reaching into the line below—have a number of meanings: first, that she is obsessional to the point of repeating an old pattern even when her logic has told her it might end in disaster! Then, they tell us that she cannot stand monotony and prefers to be in an atmosphere where the scenes are constantly changing; where there is color, novelty, music, gaiety, dancing. She has healthy, robust appetites, and a tendency to be somewhat self-indulgent, but anyone making such large formations, writing such a large hand, possesses a largesse, and thus we know there is nothing petty or small about Miss Crawford. She is an extremist and the pendulum which holds her character and personality together has wide and rhythmic swings!

In the last part of her last name, we see the sign of secretiveness, and we conclude that although she seems often direct, wholehearted, generous and outgoing, there is still much about herself she prefers not to reveal. The capital T in "Thank" is simplified, and we know from this that although Miss Crawford enjoys the fanfare, shouting and applause of a responsive audience, she has a capacity for enjoying the simple things of life, and can interpret a role depicting a simple character. Yet she is versatile enough to appear as a glamorous, exotic and unconventional creature, too. The t bar above the stem in the word "handwriting" tends to bow, and from this we deduce that she has come a long way from an earlier pattern of behavior, and that she has done this through self-development and self-discipline.

There are signs of originality in the last name, too, and we have seen her give performances which have been outstanding for their individual interpretations. Something else should be taken into consideration—considering her new position as executive of a large company: she has foresight in planning, executive ability and a capacity for cooperating with others whose judgment she respects. She possesses a strong sense of responsibility, integrity and ability to form decisions and stand staunchly by them.

JOAN CRAWFORD

Thank you for
mailing a sample of my
handwriting.

Joan Crawford

Ralph K. Davies
(U.S. Petroleum Administrator during World War II)

The angular formations in Mr. Davies' handwriting (Specimen 148) tell us that his mind is keen and that he is a reserved, sensitive individual with a good share of introversion. The main clue here to his unusual capacity to aid in constructive projects appears in the altruistic y in the word "myself" and we know that in his *giving*, his instinct to make a contribution to the world in which he moves, there is a capacity for

RALPH K. DAVIES

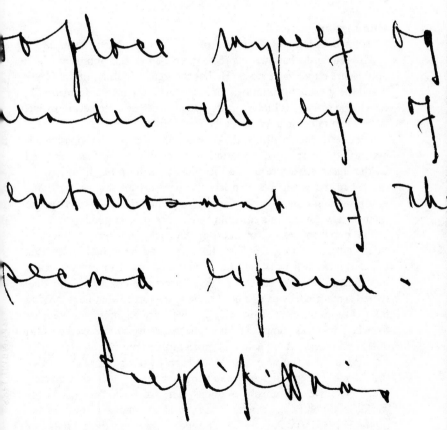

SPECIMEN 148

greatness. Twice his t bar does not go through the stem, pointing up his introversion plus a tendency to be overly cautious lest someone be hurt. Nevertheless, breaks between letters, indicating his intuition, coupled with the sign of good judgment, tell us that he *senses* when the time is ripe to be hesitant and cautious, and turns what might be a negative trait into a positive one. Often, by observing a situation, he can arrive at a more workable conclusion than if he rushed into it impulsively. Here is a man with a rich inner store of energy and abilities, which—if put to full use—could place him among the greats of our time.

Huntington Hartford
(Philanthropist and Founder of the "Handwriting Institute")

Mr. Hartford's handwriting (Specimen 149) reveals optimism which approaches euphoria at times. He has the signs of culture in the Greek d and the g made like number 8, coupled with the mental formation h, which also reveals his literary ability. That he can be extremely sensitive, at times humble, is seen in his hooked formation of the t in "most" coupled with the small capital O, while the signs of imagination together with the spiritual formation of the bowed t bar ("together") tell us that his motives are in the direction of betterment. Intuition, indicated in the breaks between letters, augments his sensitivity, giving him insight into many situations, although he often closes his eyes to the negative features in a situation and emphasizes the good.

The excellent spacing of lines on the page, with margins on both sides, indicates his capacity for organizing, and when he is convinced that his ideas will work he can muster an element of aggressiveness tempered only by his fear that he might overreach himself. The underscored signature tells us of a need to be at the top of what he is striving for and also indicates a sense of the dramatic and an inferiority complex for which he seeks compensation by making contributions to the world of art and letters. There is in him much of the simplicity of a small boy reaching out for the unattainable, and the bowed t bar again tells us that he has a deep religious feeling and a desire to curb what he considers primitive and unruly emotions. The façade he presents to the world, in which he appears to be a man of strategy (as shown by the capital H in his name), is merely a facade, for his fundamental nature is simple, modest, often childlike in its innocence. Because he is so

Dear Miss Olyanova —

I am in Palm Beach again — perhaps we can get together on my return in March. Would be most interested to see your book on handwriting when it's finished. Regards —

Hunt Hartford

SPECIMEN 149

credulous (notice the open b in "book") it has often been necessary for him to become cautious when his natural impulse has been to give lavishly. Thus, when he withholds—and this shows in the slurring of some letters and the unfinished last letters in some words—it is because of a fear which was inculcated by his environmental conditioning (during which he was overprotected), which in turn shut him away from a segment of humanity which remains foreign to him.

It becomes obvious that he has many talents which he has not, as yet, put to full use. When the protective barriers are broken down and he has only his inner resources to rely upon, he can reach the status of achievement for which he has the natural potentialities.

Helen Keller

Specimen 150, the handwriting of the woman who has become an outstanding personality because of her achievements, despite her extreme drawbacks, is not conventionally written. Yet, if we examine it closely, we will see that the formations are made artistically. The bowed stroke over the m in "sombre" tells us that she has overcome many obstacles through her religious beliefs. Persistence is revealed in the square formation of the t in "that," and all through the writing we come across original strokes apart from the Braille framework which confines her. Here the text of the specimen, not usually considered in making an analysis of handwriting, speaks volumes and might be an inspiration for others who have handicaps.

The retentive memory for which Miss Keller is famous shows in the careful dotting of her i's right above the letter, and her simple capitals tell us of her modesty as becomes the great woman we know her to be. This can be construed as an *inspirational* hand possibly *because* of the confined framework in which she is forced to function, for in any handwriting where there are so many breaks, this is the conclusion we arrive at. (Are we to conclude that the inspiration comes from her *inner sight*?)

W. Somerset Maugham

In Specimen 151, Mr. Maugham's handwriting, with its vertical angle, is that of the realist, although sometimes it seems to veer a little to the right. We see the signs of culture, intuition and acute sensitivity,

They say my
world is sombre
and drear. To me
it is warm and
joyous, and stars
shine in the dark
that cannot be
seen by day.
Cordially
Helen Keller.

SPECIMEN 150

His love had tarried for a momen
migrant bird that happens on a sh
team and for a little while folds
tired wings .

W. Somerset Maugham

SPECIMEN 151

and from the well-spaced lines on the page we know that he thinks in an organized manner. He said once that every human being he meets is another adventure, something to be explored. He is very much the keen observer with a vivid imagination, as shown in the high i dots. His tapering formations lead us to conclude that he can be smooth in his writing and tactful in his manner, yet he possesses introverted elements which keep him from mixing in a crowd. His critical faculty is clearly indicated in the tent-like i dot in the word "wings" (look at it under a magnifying glass).

He is extremely sensitive, as shown in the fairly light pen pressure, and I think he would quake inside at criticism he felt was unfair though he might not express his hurt openly. This is not what might be considered a robust hand, but there is nevertheless a capacity for persistent hard work, as shown in some long t bars. Persistence is also necessary to write entire words in one stroke without lifting the pen from the paper. Fundamentally simple, he often gets down to the core of a situation, and as we know from "Of Human Bondage" he concerns himself with the facts of life, though they be unpleasant, realistic and primitive.

Georgia O'Keeffe

Miss O'Keeffe is one of the outstanding painters on the American scene, and her handwriting (Specimen 152) shows many original formations. Written in varying angles, and done almost as though with a brush, it has signs of rhythm, sensuousness in the heavy pressure, imagination in the t bars above the stem of the letters. By her own admission her "writing varies very much with the days," and we know that she is a turbulent, intensely emotional person whose façade is one of reserve, as shown in the vertical angle of her signature.

The peculiar-looking capital M in the word "My" reveals some eccentricity in the writer, and the fact that the last stroke is more angular than the other two gives us a clue to her desire for self-assertion, and is in fact a neurotic symptom. (But then what artist is *not* neurotic ?) Her strong visual sense is seen in the broad r's, and some of her t bars tend to slant downward, telling us there is a measure of aggressiveness in her temperament. The large writing is expressive of the exaggerated forms she paints, while the lower loops, which are almost phallic-looking, and the unusually heavy pen pressure are clues to why she has chosen to give to her paintings sexual meanings. It is possible that her character could as readily be analyzed through her paintings as through her handwriting, for if you view this specimen from a distance, it may take the form of a writing made up of brush strokes.

Francis Cardinal Spellman

Primarily, this specimen of Cardinal Spellman's writing (Specimen 153) is being shown to reveal his unusual administrative and organizational ability, as indicated by the excellent spacing all around. This does not negate the fact that his rounded formations show him to be a gentle, considerate person. He is constructive in his thinking (see the printed capital R and T), practical and cautious in his planning, logical in his reasoning, with occasional flashes of intuition, and he has sound judgment in practical matters. Although sentimental, poetic

Thank you for the book.

I should have written soon but weren't feeling for a few days and forgot other things.

My writing varied very much with the day — even varied within a few pages of writing

Sincerely

Georgia O'Keeffe —

Remember, dear friends, that God gives us spiritual riches and material blessings not for ourselves alone, but to share with those who have none. Therefore I implore you to give at least one day's wage or one day's income — and pray that you may always be able to have the privilege of sharing the care of God's needy, neglected and afflicted who so desperately need your help.

Gratefully, devotedly

Francis Cardinal Spellman

SPECIMEN 153

and outgoing, as shown in the combination of the right slant, rounded formations and signs of imagination in the t bar above the stem, he also has the kind of caution that businessmen have. This is shown in the closed small b ("blessings"). We also know that he can be firm in his convictions—note the final stroke in the word "God." The clue to his religious status is evident in the cross made horizontally in the first and looped stroke of his signature. The rest of his signature is simple and modest, showing his sincerity as a prelate.

Selman A. Waksman
(Discoverer of Streptomycin)

Dr. Waksman's handwriting (Specimen 154) shows his scientific mind and capacity for logical reasoning. There are the signs of self-

SELMAN A. WAKSMAN

My dear Miss Olganova:

I am in receipt of your letter. I hasten to write a few words, as your request. If this is postponed, I may never come back to it.

I hope that these lines will give you the necessary material to work with.

With best wishes

Sincerely yours

Selman A. Waksman

discipline (without which no scientist could achieve anything). The first capital I is distinguished by being so small, showing his modesty and tendency to be self-effacing. Some words are very small, others larger, and we see here a conflict between the intellect and emotions. In the end, the intellect wins, for it manages to sit in judgment on the feelings and control them for a time.

The varying angles tell us of a person whose moods change. When he is working, he is withdrawn and isolated; when socializing, his need for people makes him friendly and outgoing. Evident talent shows in both the printed capital and small s, and his intuition, shown in many breaks in words, indicates that he has insights which are developed as a result of his observations. There is more to Dr. Waksman than meets the eye, with the variety of t bars as well as the different angles and size of letters, but we are concerned here with the scientist who has made a valuable contribution to the welfare of the world. In him there are still untapped resources. His excellent memory shows in the careful dotting of his i's, while the angularity of so many of his letters tells us that he is keen-minded and rather exacting in his work, but also that he has changing moods which yank him in different directions and which he hides under a mask of reserve. He is a man who is not afraid to be human, and he reveals himself spontaneously when he is with people who speak his language.

Ted Williams

Intelligent, warm, friendly and outgoing, Ted Williams reveals himself in his handwriting (Specimen 155). He is extremely sensitive, as might be expected from someone with so vivid an imagination—revealed in high i dots coupled with t bars above the stems. The t bars bow, too, giving us a clue to a spiritual (or is it mystical?) quality. But they also disclose his capacity for curbing impulses which might take him far afield. In these t bars, we recognize the sign of the perfectionist, the dreamer, the individual who reaches out for the unattainable, for something beyond concrete reality. They are also a clue to his rich world of fantasy, but in this he is balanced by good judgment —note the y which comes down in a single stroke instead of a loop. It tells us that he can keep his feet safely on the ground even when his head may be in the clouds.

Examining the handwriting further, we see other t bar formations.

Somerset Hotel 400 COMMONWEALTH AVENUE · BOSTON 15

Dear Mr Olyanova,

Sorry I'm so late with a reply to your letter.

Hope this is what you want

Sincerely.

Ted Williams

Nadya Olyanova

98 Horatio St,

New York 14, N.Y.

There is a minus one in the word "this" which we have come to recognize as a neurotic sign. In one area of his emotional structure, he has not completely grown up and has moments of indecision, hesitance, passivity. But then there are a number of t bars which are lance-like, and we know from these that he can be terse, sarcastic, at times argumentative and on the defensive. This is confirmed by the downward stroke of the t bar in the word "want" and we must remember that this is also the sign of the rebel. Ted Williams will fight for what he believes is right, when he feels an injustice has been done him—or others. If he appears to have a chip on his shoulder, this is part of his defense mechanism, invented to cover up an inner pliability. He has learned to guard against being taken in by his softer feelings so that his outer crust is his safeguard.

Although the rising lines reveal optimism, this is modified by the word "you" which tends to slant downward, and from the combination we deduce that he has moods of self-doubt and depression. This does not prevent him from keeping his eye "on the ball" (or goal), and this is also true realistically, as shown in the broad r's which reveal his strong visual sense.

His capital D, open at the top, tells us he can be frank and outspoken as well as openhearted. The original and graceful turn of his y's reminds us of the graceful gestures he often makes on the baseball field.

His signature is in harmony with the rest of his writing and from this we know that his personality is in a harmonious balance with his character. The hook on the lower part of the capital T in his first name shows not only tenacity but a measure of clannishness. The over-all picture is of a man who has overcome many ups and downs in his life and can stand firmly on his own feet.

Notice the involved capital H in "Horatio." We talked of this as the sign of the strategist and conclude that our baseball hero occasionally gets himself into tight situations but possesses the foresight, judgment, and tenacity to get himself out of them. And if he is interfered with, he will fight for his rights. By the same token, he will also defend his loved ones if they are threatened, for he is a man who needs affection, understanding and warmth—to which he will respond much more readily than he would to force, pressure or obvious domination.

25. Graphology and Standard Psychological Tests

By George E. Edington and Bradford J. Wilson

Many people have asked how graphology stands up beside other standard "tests" of personality. Professionals who use these tests in their work, as well as laymen, have wondered whether handwriting analysis compared favorably with such techniques as the Rorschach, Thematic Apperception Test (TAT) and the Wechsler Adult Intelligence Scale (WAIS). It is not easy to answer this, because each of these instruments measures personality from a different standpoint. The WAIS, for example, was designed specifically to get at various phases of thinking and reasoning, all of which come under the general heading of "intelligence." The TAT, on the other hand, is a picture interpretation test that uses storytelling to discover how a person sees and reacts to various phases of living. The Rorschach ink blot method is based on the assumption that a person reveals general personality trends through what he sees in ink blots.

Each of these tests goes well beyond its original design in the amount of information it can give us about the person being tested. Graphology and the Rorschach, however, seem to come closest to each other in measuring the same personality characteristics.

Ink blot pictures, of course, were not new with Rorschach. Making them had been a pleasant parlor game. Blots had also been used more seriously by psychiatrists, along with cloud pictures, to help patients verbalize by giving them a starting point for their ideas. These ideas could in turn lead to a more insightful discussion of a patient's problems. Rorschach, however, made a unique discovery. He found that responses to the ink blots could be coded or "scored." He noted with each response *how much* of the blot was used, *what characteristics* of the blot seemed most important to the patient—its form, texture, color—and the *kind* of things that were seen. Certain patterns began to emerge from this scored material which coincided with certain types of personalities. Using thousands of subjects with known personality features, he built up an important body of knowledge. Today an examiner trained to use the test as Rorschach and others have developed it can reliably predict an individual's major personality characteristics.

The Rorschach test as we know it today consists of ten ink blots which Dr. Rorschach had found were most likely to evoke responses. Since his day, careful workers in the field of clinical psychology have studied it, enriched it, and expanded its use in different aspects until it is now a refined and flexible instrument. As a result, considerable use has been made of the test, especially in the United States.

The scoring of the Rorschach is only a kind of shorthand which is still crude in some of its aspects. In order for the psychologist to use the test accurately, he must look at the *total* record and its content as well as the scored material. The finer and sometimes crucial details are frequently derived only from close attention to each individual response. The purpose of "scoring" *any* kind of psychological material is simply to boil it down so that its quantity and quality can be compared with other similar material. As an analogy, if we know that a certain cup of coffee contains one spoonful of sugar and an ounce of cream, we can compare it with a cup that has a saccharine pill and no cream at all. If we examine enough cups of coffee, we can find out what most people drink (as is done in market research). Gradually we discover the things which are common, and the things which are quite unusual or even bizarre (such as finding a cup of coffee with a teaspoon of corn flakes in it). Scoring is the best technique yet developed for diagramming abstract material. If it fails to give adequate information, the fault lies in the particular scoring system used, not in the mere fact that somebody tried to score abstract material.

When the objection is raised, as it often is, that "you can't *score* a human personality," what the speaker really means is "*I* can't score such complicated data." One might as well say "you can't score human blood"—but it is done in the laboratory every day. All reality is measurable, provided one can invent the appropriate tools for measuring it.

In Rorschach, the scoring techniques so far developed are continually being checked and rechecked for accuracy with, we might add, a certain amount of frustration and disagreement. And yet the scored material is essential for making comparisons between two or more records.

Let's return to the original question: how does graphology compare with Rorschach? The answer is complicated by the fact that both instruments depend for their accuracy on the examiner's depth of interest in human beings—his sensitivity to their needs, desires and aspirations. As for a point-by-point comparison of the two methods, no extensive studies have been done in this area. The fact that there is as yet no definite scoring system for handwriting analysis makes it difficult to begin such an undertaking.

Every graphologist, in a sense, develops his own equivalent of scoring techniques in the way in which he first appraises the over-all aspect of the sample before him, and in the steps he follows thereafter. Klara Roman, Werner Wolff and others have devised lists of personality factors to be considered and graphological indicators to be taken into account in arriving at conclusions. But these are more in the nature of thorough checklists than actual scoring systems in themselves. From the material in this book, you may be able to construct your own system if you wish. *

While graphology and the Rorschach both measure essentially the same factors, some personality features appear to stand out more clearly and distinctly in one than in the other. A glance at a handwriting sample, for example, is often sufficient to tell us whether the writer is extravagant, grandiose, or careful and detailed in his everyday life—facts not always evident in the Rorschach. The Rorschach, on the other hand, often gives us almost at a glance the guiding fantasies of the individual. We know from some of the handwriting "signs" how much a person indulges in fantasy—wide spreading upper loops, distorted forms in the upper zone, and so forth, will tell us that daydreams are

---

* We are attempting to construct a system of weighted scores to be correlated with the Rorschach and WAIS. In doing this we have found the specificity of Miss Olyanova's indicators particularly useful. For example, the chief indicators of fantasy activity in handwriting are to be found in the formation of t bars. Miss Olyanova's work in this area alone throws much needed light on this important aspect of interpretation. The observations she makes about t bars also apply to other upper zone formations, as well as to similar gestures when they occur elsewhere in the handwriting. Perhaps the most important characteristic of Miss Olyanova's techniques in general is that they are so largely a product of her long experience analyzing not hundreds, but thousands of handwritings. Not content to follow obediently in the footsteps of her teachers, she has had the vision to formulate many new theories based on her own rich and varied experience.

important to the writer. Loops so high that they tangle with the line above will characterize an individual who acts out his Walter Mitty dreams in daily activities. But very seldom are we able to get a good idea from the sample itself of the content of these daydreams. More often than not, the Rorschach response will tell us what the subject thinks about in his fantasies and how he feels about such thoughts—proud, ashamed, secretive, as the case may be.

Handwriting may alert us to the fact that we are dealing with a timid or apprehensive individual—one who may be startled by every ripple of curtains in the breeze. But the specific nature as well as the probable cause of such fears is more often evident in the Rorschach than in the handwriting. At the same time, handwriting is most apt to reveal the way in which the writer actually *behaves*. In a Rorschach situation, the subject imposes his inner view of life upon a more or less unstructured blot. This in itself has little practical relevance to everyday tasks, even though we are able to infer a great many things from his reactions and can get numerous clues to how he *might* live from day to day.

In contrast to this, the task of writing is a fairly ordinary one, frequently performed by most people. The person who takes the Rorschach knows that he is being tested, and he may try to give the "right answers" despite all the examiner's efforts to keep the proceedings relaxed and spontaneous. Handwriting, however, is so much a part of everyday living that even when the subject knows the sample is to be evaluated, he seldom makes any effort to disguise or "improve" his hand. For this reason it is more habitual, and in a sense more characteristic of the person than his response to a set of unfamiliar blots. This is especially true of literal, practical, unartistic individuals who are not at home with abstractions. These people may show lethargy, disinterest, bafflement or impatience on the Rorschach and prove to be alert and resourceful on the WAIS. But their handwriting will indicate at one glance both their impatience with abstraction and their emphasis on practical common sense. When an individual writes, he is performing an act, tracing a pathway, making gestures. The contrasts between his thinking and acting will become quite apparent. Therefore, handwriting is comparable to the two basic parts of the WAIS—the verbal and performance sections—which measure thinking and acting. In addition, the way in which these two factors interact will be more apparent in the handwriting sample. (It should be made clear that in this context we are referring to handwriting which is written for others to read—not to scribbled jottings, school notes, and self-reminders intended only for the writer himself.)

A difficulty which arises in comparing various systems of personality evaluation is that very few people are trained in *both* handwriting analysis and Rorschach, let alone handwriting and the other tests. Added to this, there is a different tradition with each test. In the field of psychology, the emphasis on what psychologists think is important has changed. At one time it was thought that "criminality" was a personality factor by itself and that certain qualities of personality were confined to the "antisocial person." Today we know that criminality may arise from a great many causes. We once examined a number of "Wanted by the F.B.I." notices on a post office wall, selecting those in which the crime involved murder. Since signatures were given on each card, we had a handwriting sample of sorts to work with. Even from the signature alone it became evident that one man had murdered because of a violent and uncontrolled temper, while another was psychotic and may not have known what he was doing. Others were so-called "psychopathic personalities" for whom murder (during an attempted robbery, for instance) appeared the easiest way of dealing with a situation. Even in the Rorschach test itself, emphasis has changed. Dr. Rorschach believed that his test was a good measure of "introversion" and "extroversion," and while this is a factor that may still be derived from the test it is not, in the United States at least, considered of crucial importance.

Handwriting analysis, of course, does not have the advantage of developing from a common source with a single clinical tradition as the Rorschach does. The various "schools" of graphology—French, German, Swiss—differ somewhat from one another. However, the emphasis in handwriting has usually been placed on factors which the writer himself may be aware of. Furthermore, graphology, much older than Rorschach, has been used by many people both inside and outside the field of psychology. The Rorschach is almost invariably studied along with or subsequent to other psychological techniques. Most important of all, it grew up in a clinical atmosphere for the purpose of measuring pathological states. Graphology, on the other hand, was developed in order to assess normal variations in personality. It has been said of Rorschach reports that they still tend to emphasize malignancies rather than strengths and resources. This seems to be due more to the training of the particular clinician than to the nature of the instrument itself. Since handwriting analyses are often prepared for the subjects themselves, graphologists have *had* to learn to recognize many more signs of strength, resourcefulness and potential talent than have clinicians, who are still conscientiously investigating these elements in projective tests.

In the final analysis, the comparison between graphology and standard diagnostic tests rests largely upon the psychological background as well as the experience and sensitivity which the examiner brings to his task. The proof of the pudding in this case is in the final report which he submits, and its relevance to the individual and his needs. It is not necessary for either the psychologist or the graphologist to predict what a person likes for breakfast, or whether he prefers blondes to brunettes. But it is reasonable to ask that a well-rounded portrait in depth be produced when it is called for.

A good report, from the psychologist's point of view, should include information on the following areas. First, intelligence—and by this we mean the subject's ability to reason, to concentrate, to use logic, to plan and to learn, as well as the originality of his thinking, his ability to be abstract, his rote memory, and his ability to put his thinking to practical everyday uses. Personal relationships are important, and these include all his dealings with other people—the general public, acquaintances, close friends, and the people he loves. Then we may ask about the strength of his emotional control. Is he impulsive or cautious, both in relation to his inner excitements and to the things that go on around him? What about the picture he has of himself? Does he look upon himself as an ugly duckling, a prince in disguise or an ordinary Joe—and to what extent does he hide or reveal this in his everyday life? Special problems, special abilities and talents should be covered in a report. When diagnosis is called for, an attempt should be made to outline any possible factors that will aid or hinder the subject's response to therapy and the productive unfolding of his personality.

It would take an entire book to elaborate upon the various ways in which a clinical psychologist, on the one hand, and a skilled graphologist, on the other, might arrive at essentially the same conclusions. Just as clinicians may vary in background, philosophy and the theoretical framework onto which they "hang" their material, so there can be similar variations from one graphologist to another. Given a graphologist and a psychologist who have the same backgrounds, and provided they are both interested in obtaining the same kind of information about the same areas of personality, the reports should coincide in all essential respects. Otherwise one can expect to find the kind of variation between the psychologist and the graphologist that might exist among psychologists themselves, or among individual graphologists.

A final point of comparison should be noted. The Rorschach and other psychodiagnostic tests must be learned under personal supervision if the student is to acquire any proficiency in their use. This is largely because of the complexities of administration and scoring. It would be difficult to imagine anyone learning to interpret the Rorschach or WAIS from books alone. Graphology, on the other hand, has the advantage of being administered without special tools, it requires no scoring, and the techniques of interpretation can often be succinctly stated, as they are in this book.

Because handwriting is so much a part of our day-to-day experience, we are apt to understand a great deal more about it than we consciously realize. Thus when we undertake the formal study of graphology, we may bring to our learning a lifetime of unconscious observation of the handwritings of people familiar to us, or whose chief characteristics are well known. In contrast to this, it takes literally years and a great deal of effort for a psychologist using the other tests to acquire the kind of experience that every beginning graphologist often has at his disposal.

Despite the differences in training methods, both clinical psychology and graphology rely heavily upon the individual's intuitive ability to draw subtle and accurate conclusions from the techniques he has learned. As holds true for so many things, it is this quality of intuition which makes the difference between competence and talent. In this volume Miss Olyanova has provided the tools for both—the rest is up to you.